DUKE

THE MUSICAL LIFE OF DUKE ELLINGTON

DUKE

THE MUSICAL LIFE OF DUKE ELLINGTON

by Bill Gutman

Random House · New York

Library of Congress Cataloging in Publication Data
Gutman, Bill.   Duke: the musical life of Duke Ellington.
SUMMARY: A biography of the pianist, composer, and band leader who popularized jazz.   1. Elling-
ton, Duke, 1899–1974—Juvenile literature.   2. Composers—Biography—Juvenile literature.
[1. Ellington, Duke, 1899–1974.   2. Musicians.   3. Afro-Americans—Biography]   I. Title.
ML410.E44G9   785.4'2'0924 [B] [92]   76–8138
ISBN 0–394–83097–0   *Designed by Murray M. Herman*
Manufactured in the United States of America   2 3 4 5 6 7 8 9 0

PHOTOGRAPH CREDITS: CBS Records, 1; Michael Lee, 174 (top and bottom); Pictorial Parade, Inc.,
7 (Paris Match), 144 (AFP), 145 (top), 158 (London Daily Express); RCA Records, 76 (bottom),
109; The Collection of Duncan Schiedt, 46, 47, 74, 75, 76 (top), 77, 107 (bottom), 108 (top); United
Press International, 2, 48, 108 (bottom), 156; U.S. Department of State, 145 (bottom); Wide World
Photos, Inc., 107 (top), 157.

Acknowledgments

When writing about a man like Duke Ellington, it is difficult to cite all of those who have contributed to keeping his work, as well as his memory, alive. There are numerous persons connected both directly and indirectly with Duke and his world who have helped make this book possible. To begin with, there are the many, many musicians—some who gave themselves and their talents to Duke and others who gave to the jazz community at large. Then there are those behind the scenes—family, friends, writers, critics, recording people, and fans—whose love and appreciation of Duke and his music have added to the ever-growing collection of Ellington memorabilia. And no list of acknowledgments would be complete without a full expression of indebtedness to the man himself, Edward Kennedy Ellington, for having lived, worked, and inspired so many people.

The author would also like to give very special thanks to the following men for personally sharing with him their recollections and feelings about Duke Ellington: Stanley Dance, Billy Taylor, Brooks Kerr, Russell Procope, and Pastor John Gensel.

Grateful acknowledgment is made for permission
to reprint excerpts from the following works:

From MUSIC IS MY MISTRESS by Duke Ellington. Copyright © 1973 by Duke Ellington, Inc. Reprinted by permission of Doubleday & Company, Inc.

Since this page cannot legibly accommodate all necessary permissions acknowledgments, they are continued on the following page.

For Elizabeth

Other books containing information about Duke Ellington:

BIG BAND JAZZ by Albert McCarthy, G. P. Putnam's Sons, 1974.

EARLY JAZZ: ITS ROOTS AND MUSICAL DEVELOPMENT by Gunther Schuller, Oxford University Press, 1968.

Contents

1

The Duke

In April 1969 the President of the United States stood before a large gathering of more than a hundred people in the elegant ballroom of the White House. He raised his glass and told his audience that in the past he had toasted ambassadors, prime ministers, kings, and queens, but this was the first time he had ever toasted a duke. The duke accepted the toast graciously, bowing in the direction of his host. Then, smiling broadly, he kissed the surprised President twice on each cheek.

The duke was not a visiting dignitary from a foreign country. He was a black man born in Washington, D.C.—Edward Kennedy "Duke" Ellington, one of the greatest figures in the history of American music. The gala White House party was being held in honor of his seventieth birthday. And that evening President Richard M. Nixon presented Duke Ellington with the Presidential Medal of Freedom, the highest award the United States government can bestow upon a civilian.

But the highlight of the evening was the music, mostly Duke Ellington's music, a music called jazz. Scores of prominent jazz musicians, along with many government officials, had been invited to the party. Most of them knew Duke, and all of them loved his music. Eagerly, the musicians took turns performing the music that Duke had been giving the world for some fifty years. And once they started they were hard to stop. Even after President and Mrs. Nixon had retired for the night, the formal White House ballroom rocked with the swinging rhythms of a jam session—until the wee hours of the morning.

Duke himself spent a great deal of time at the piano that night, sometimes sharing the spotlight with other greats of the jazz world. For a while he sat next to his friend and teacher Willie "the Lion" Smith and cheered the older pianist on.

"The big moment for me," Duke said later, "was when I saw my man, the Lion, playing the President's grand piano with his derby on his head!"

How was it that this man, Duke Ellington, was chosen to be honored by the President of the United States and given his country's highest civilian award? Fifty years earlier the same Duke had been a clerk in a government office in Washington who spent his spare time organizing dance bands to make a little extra money for himself.

In those days a new music was just beginning to develop. It was a music that would eventually become known as jazz, but was then considered low and vulgar by most respectable people. It was a music that had grown directly out of the experience of black people in America, played and sung wherever black people lived and worked. And Duke Ellington, proud of his black heritage, loved that music. Perhaps no other musician was as important to its growth and development.

Duke became a prominent jazz pianist in his own right. But he was also one of the most important composers and arrangers to have worked in the idiom. For fifty years he managed to keep a large orchestra together through good and bad times, using the band as his mode of expression, an instrument to play his compositions. In doing so he helped create a whole new world of sound.

During Duke Ellington's long career, the new music slowly emerged from the saloons and cabarets, made its way into the dance palaces and night clubs, and eventually climbed onto the concert stage. Jazz had great popular appeal—to young and old, black and white, rich and poor alike. In time, jazz became universally recognized as a legitimate art form, and some contend it is the only art form to have originated on American soil.

Duke Ellington remained in the forefront of the new music for more than half a century. By the 1960s, Duke was an unofficial ambassador of the United States, traveling with his band to every corner of the world. On tours sponsored by the United States Department of State, they played in Russia, Japan, Latin America, the Far East, the Middle East, and Africa. Wherever they went, jazz was recognized not only as a form of black expression but also as a unique form of American expression.

Duke himself was a man of elegance and mystery. In the early days of jazz, when many whites looked down on the black man and his music, Duke Ellington brought grace and dignity to every performance. Jazz historian Leonard Feather once described Ellington the public figure: "An inch over six feet tall, sturdily built, he had an innate grandeur that would have enabled him to step with unquenched dignity out of a mud puddle. His phrasing of an announcement, the elegance of his diction, the supreme courtesy of his bow, whether to a duchess in

London or a theater audience in Des Moines, lent stature not only to his own career, but to the whole world of jazz."

Duke's private life was not as easy to describe. He was something of an enigma. It is known that he spent much of his time writing and arranging music for his band. And although he had many friends, none of them ever came to know the whole man. He always kept a part of himself in the shadows, revealing only as much to a person as he desired. He could be friendly and personable, but he also jealously guarded his privacy, perhaps because he had so little of it.

It is Duke's music that is most important to us, because that was what was most important to him. His fertile imagination led him to write many kinds of music, from three-minute tunes for recording sessions, to elaborate suites for concert performance, to music for revues and films. And finally, he developed an original form of sacred music for performance in churches.

Duke attracted some of the country's greatest jazz musicians to his side. Then, through the innovative arranging techniques he employed, he proceeded to bring out the very best in each of them. In fact, his arrangements are almost impossible to duplicate because they depend on the individual talents of his musicians.

Duke hated categories, and indeed his music is difficult to categorize. He himself preferred not to call it jazz. Each time a critic thought he had placed Duke in the proper slot, Duke would head off in a new direction.

After the White House party broke up, sometime around 2 A.M., Duke did not take time to relax and savor the occasion. He rushed back to his hotel, changed from his formal attire into his traveling clothes, and raced to the airport to catch an early-morning flight to Oklahoma City. The Ellington band would perform there that night, and Duke would be out front, leading them as usual. For despite all his success as a composer, and all the honors he received for his contributions to music, Duke was still a working musician. Even at seventy, with forty years of constant travel behind him, he was still on the road.

In Oklahoma City he would bound out on stage to greet a new audience of fans. He would announce the numbers, introduce his great musicians, then play introductions and solos at the piano. His band would play the old standards, his many hit tunes, as well as new, experimental pieces.

When the show was over, Duke would bow graciously and assure the audience, as he did after every performance, "We all love you . . . madly." Shortly he and the group would be off again, heading for the next stop. And riding through the dark, whether by car or bus or plane, Duke would be working on the next tune, the next arrangement, the next suite. For he always looked to the future, and he never ran out of ideas. Some five years later, desperately ill in a New York City hospital, he was still turning out new compositions for the band.

Duke Ellington's career spanned the whole history of jazz. And nowhere in that glorious history is there a man who had more love for his music, more respect for his art, than the man they called the Duke.

2

"Music for All Occasions"

Edward Kennedy Ellington was born in Washington, D.C., on April 29, 1899. His parents, James Edward and Daisy Kennedy Ellington, were a hard-working couple who showered their first child with love and affection. Edward was brought up as an only child. His only sister, Ruth, was born when he was sixteen years old, an accomplished young man in high school. His friends were already calling him "Duke," and the nickname suited his personality so well that it became almost a given name. For the rest of his life he was "Duke" Ellington to all but his family and closest friends.

The times were very different from today in 1899. America was just 123 years old and approaching a new century. William McKinley was President, women were not yet allowed to vote, people didn't have to pay income taxes. There were no airplanes, very few automobiles, no radio or television. The phonograph and silent movies were brand-new inventions few people had seen.

Although the absence of our modern machines made the times slower and more relaxed, for most people work was harder and work hours were longer. Laborers worked twelve hours a day six days a week—and still had a hard time earning enough to put food on their tables.

The Ellington family was black, and in Washington at the turn of the century that made a big difference. Blacks were paid less money even if they did the same jobs as white people. There were no black congressmen and very few blacks in the business world. Most worked as porters, janitors, waiters, maids, butlers, chauffeurs, bootblacks, street cleaners.

The Civil War, which had ended thirty-four years earlier, resulted in an end to slavery. But law and custom kept black people apart from white people, especially in the South. Blacks lived in separate neighborhoods and were forbidden by law to eat in the same restaurants as whites, stay in the same hotels, sit in the same section of a theater, even use the same drinking fountain. The law also required that black and white children attend separate schools.

The Ellingtons shared with other black people the discrimination and lack of opportunity. But they were among the upper levels of black society. Duke's father, "J.E.," was a jovial, happy man who managed to provide very well for his family. When he was still in his teens, Mr. Ellington had gone to work for a well-known Washington doctor, M.F. Cuthbert, who lived in one of the most fashionable parts of the city. J.E. eventually became Dr. Cuthbert's butler and a close friend as well.

While he continued as a butler, Duke's father learned to be a caterer, preparing and serving food at some of Washington's most important social functions. He served on special occasions at the White House and at many of the embassies and ministries throughout the capital.

Although J.E. didn't make a great deal of money, his family lived comfortably. And he was able to keep his own home stocked with the finest foods available, contributing to many glorious family meals and parties.

As Duke himself recalled in his autobiography, *Music Is My Mistress:* "J.E. always acted as though he had money, whether he had it or not. He spent and lived like a man who had money, and he raised his family as though he were a millionaire."

Daisy Ellington wasn't as outgoing as her husband. In fact, she appeared to be rather stern and tight-lipped, despite her striking beauty. During Duke's first years, his mother was with him constantly, as were his grandmother and several aunts, leading him to admit he was "spoiled rotten" by all the women in his family.

His mother was a religious woman, with a strong belief that there was a divine presence in her life. "My mother started telling me about God when I was very young," he wrote in his autobiography. "There was never any talk about red people, brown people, black people, or yellow people, or about the differences that existed between them."

Duke said his mother constantly painted wonderful word pictures of God. On Sundays she would take him to at least two churches. Those early religious experiences gave him a feeling of security and a belief that he was a very special kind of child. His mother often told him that he would have nothing to worry about in life because he was blessed.

Both of Duke's parents had a strong sense of their own self worth. And they taught their son to carry himself with dignity and poise. Those who knew him as a boy recall that he always seemed to have the same natural sense of confidence he would show years later as a performer.

As Duke grew older, he gained a sense of pride in his race and a desire to learn more about his heritage as a black man. The principal of his school, Miss Boston, reinforced the sense of pride Duke had gotten from his parents. She "would explain the importance of proper speech," he wrote. "It would be most important in our lives to come. When we went out into the world, we would have the grave responsibility of being practically always on stage, for every time people saw a Negro, they would go into a reappraisal of the race. . . . This being an all-colored school, Negro history was crammed into the curriculum, so that we would know our people all the way back. They had pride there, the greatest race pride. . . ."

Duke's black pride and his knowledge of black history would one day help shape his music. He would come to see jazz as music that grew out of the black experience.

Soon after Duke started grade school at age five, he was drawn to sports. Major league baseball had just come to Washington, and Duke and his friends followed the Senators. They hung around the ball park whenever they could, and after school they would play ball until dinner, sometimes on an old tennis court not far from the White House. On more than one occasion President Theodore Roosevelt would ride up on a horse, pause, and watch the boys play for a few minutes.

"When he got ready to go," Duke recalled, "he would wave and we would wave at him."

Duke's mother let him play ball, but she encouraged

him to do other things as well. When he was seven she began sending him for piano lessons several times a week. His teacher had the appropriate name of Mrs. Clinkscales. Duke wasn't a child prodigy. In fact, he hated the lessons and did all he could to avoid them. He would rather have been out playing ball with his friends.

"At this point, piano was not my recognized talent," Duke admitted. "After all, baseball, football, track, and athletics were what the real he-men were identified with, and so they were naturally the most important to me."

Duke made his first appearance as a pianist at a church concert given by Mrs. Clinkscales and her students. Though his teacher and parents praised his efforts, Duke's mind was elsewhere. He got no satisfaction from playing the piano. Gradually he drifted away from music and soon forgot almost everything Mrs. Clinkscales had taught him.

When Duke was twelve, his older cousin Sonny Ellington became, in Duke's words, "companion, advisor, bodyguard, and confidant." On Sundays, the two boys would walk all through Washington, visiting their many relatives, stopping for a meal at each place. This was one of the benefits of having a large family—a meal at every port. The boys quickly worked off the endless flow of food by more walking and general horsing around.

Life with Sonny was also an education of sorts. The older boy had many friends, friends who were wise to the ways of the streets. Sonny bought pulp magazines and passed them around for everyone else to read. Duke, the youngest, was the last to get them, but he read them intently—perhaps because he knew his parents wouldn't approve of their violent stories about cowboys and detectives.

Duke and his friends sometimes got into fights with other boys from nearby neighborhoods, some black, some white. These scraps were potentially dangerous, though Duke was never really hurt except for bumps and bruises. None of these incidents left him with any permanent bitterness, possibly since his family life was basically good and happy.

Duke didn't spend all his spare time on the streets. In his early teens he got a summer job as a vendor at the Washington Senators' ball park. Shouting for the attention of a large crowd gave him his first case of stage fright. But he was proud that by the end of the season he'd been promoted from popcorn and peanuts to the more prestigious cold drinks.

His next job led to a whole new experience. The summer before he entered high school, he went with his mother to Asbury Park, New Jersey, a seaside resort. As soon as he arrived, he started looking for a job.

Though Duke was only fifteen years old, he looked older. As he went around to the big hotels on the ocean, asking for employment, he learned there was a dishwasher's job open. When he applied, the woman in charge of the kitchen said he could have the job.

The headwaiter, Bowser, took a liking to Duke and offered to teach him the right way to wash dishes. Duke didn't think he needed teaching. He unsuspectingly plunged his hands into the scalding water and pulled them out twice as fast. Then he accepted instruction and became friends with Bowser. Before long their conversation turned to music. Bowser loved piano music and told Duke about a young piano player named Harvey Brooks, who was playing down in Philadelphia.

"He's just about your age," Bowser said, "and you ought to hear him play. He's terrific."

So after the whole summer in Asbury Park, on the way home to Washington, Duke stopped with Bowser in Philadelphia and heard Harvey Brooks, who was only eighteen. Duke, writing in his autobiography, remembered the impression young Brooks made on him: "He was swinging, and he had a tremendous left hand, and when I got home I had a real yearning to play. I hadn't been able to get off the ground before, but after hearing him I said to myself, 'Man, you're just going to *have* to do it.' "

In a way, hearing Harvey was the beginning of Duke's musical life. Since his early piano lessons with Mrs. Clinkscales, he had hardly touched the piano. He hadn't much liked the instrument. But now, Duke suddenly wanted to play. He went home to Washington determined to take up the piano again.

That fall Edward Kennedy Ellington became "Duke" Ellington. One of his friends, Edgar McEntree, decided Edward should have a title. McEntree settled on *Duke*, and the name stuck. Even as a teen-ager, Ellington seemed to fit the name perfectly. In high school, Duke was something of a dandy. Tall, trim, and good-looking, he always wore a tie, always had his shoes shined and spotless. He had a deep, resonant voice, and his bearing was elegant.

Armstrong High was an all-black school specializing in training students for a manual trade. Duke enrolled there in 1914 with the idea of studying freehand and mechanical drawing. And for a while art seemed to be his major talent. He won a poster contest sponsored by the National Association for the Advancement of Colored People. And he often made plaques and posters for various events around the school. Duke always designed his posters and plaques with an eye toward their commercial value. Because he was a young black man, he felt it was very important to find a way of making a living. He knew the doors of many places would be closed, so a kind of practical skill was a necessity.

Duke's other subjects often bored him, and he skipped classes whenever he felt like it. Only two subjects held his interest—art and music. Soon he was practicing on the piano as much as he worked at his drawing. Often he would sit in some of his less interesting classes and run his hands back and forth across an imaginary keyboard on his desk.

The music bug had bitten him. Duke began studying piano with "Doc" Perry and music theory with Henry Grant, who taught both in the high schools and privately. Duke was a promising student, quick to master the fundamentals and eager to experiment with new things. Soon he could turn simple exercises into adventures by improvising—playing a melody with new variations each time. Grant later taught theory to two young men named Otto Hardwick and Arthur Whetsol, who would one day be members of the early Ellington band.

Duke was also exploring the world outside of school. And as his prowess at the piano increased, so did his popularity. He and his friends lied about their ages to get into burlesque shows, where music, comedy, and variety acts were presented—along with beautiful girls in brief costumes. He never forgot the show-business techniques of burlesque shows and "the rather gorgeous girls, who looked good in anything they wore."

Then there was Frank Holliday's poolroom, another favorite hangout, a place Duke and his friends had been visiting since they were about fourteen. The poolroom was a meeting place for many types of people—gamblers and hustlers, law and medical students, Pullman porters and dining-car waiters. The gamblers sometimes showed the boys the tricks they used to cheat other players. Pickpockets from New York boasted that they had been forbidden to use the new subways there because of their skills.

Piano players also came to Frank Holliday's, to take their turns at the old piano in the corner. Most of them are forgotten now, but Duke listened carefully and picked up many little tricks from them. Some of the musicians played professionally, others for kicks. Some were highly educated, having studied at music conservatories. Others didn't know a half note from an arpeggio and couldn't read music. But their fingers produced magic on the keyboard.

"There was a wonderful thing, an exchange, which went on between them," Duke wrote. "I used to spend nights listening to Doc Perry, Louis Brown, and Louis Thomas. They were schooled musicians who had been to the conservatory. But I listened to the unschooled, too. There was a fusion, a borrowing of ideas, and they helped one another right in front of where I was standing, leaning over the piano, listening. Oh, I was a great listener!"

One of the poolroom pianists, Doc Perry, became Duke's

first important piano teacher. Perry spent endless hours showing Duke various techniques and tricks. He never asked for payment of any kind. Duke's enthusiasm was enough. All of his learning was by ear. Few of the musicians ever thought of writing anything down. So to learn a piece, Duke had to fix the harmonies and the melody in his head—memorize the tune on the spot. He said many years later that he learned his "primitive system of memorizing" during these sessions and used it for the rest of his career.

Duke was still in high school, but more and more of his interests lay outside its doors. No longer was his music a sometime hobby; it was becoming an all-consuming passion.

He began traveling around to so-called rent parties, where guests were charged a small admission fee and had to pay for their drinks. The hosts used the money to pay their rent. Pianists came to these parties just for a chance to play for an appreciative audience. And young musicians such as Ellington came to listen. Since none of the new music was written down or recorded, a student had to hear his favorites play live. As soon as Duke left a party he headed for the nearest piano and tried to duplicate the chords and melodies he had heard. Slowly his own technique and style began to take shape.

Although Duke wasn't a featured player at the rent parties, his friends already urged him to play whenever they got together. He would go through the few pieces he knew, varying the tempo and the beat, making one tune sound like two or three. His first original composition was a simple ragtime piece that he called "Soda Fountain Rag," because he had worked after school as a soda jerk.

Before long, Duke was being asked to play for pay. While still in high school he began playing as a member of ragtime pianist Louis Thomas's "gig" bands. Thomas had several groups that he sent on various one-night playing engagements in different parts of the city. Thomas played with his best band and sent his second- and third-string groups to less important engagements. Thomas offered Duke a job with his least accomplished band if he could learn a number called "The Siren Song." Duke learned it in one day.

He was ready for "The Siren Song," but little else. While the other musicians talked about chord changes and all the tunes they planned to play, Duke sat at the piano in a state of shock. Then someone requested the one number he knew. He went into his act, improvising on "Siren Song" and delighting the crowd. But he knew he was just faking it, getting by on a little flash, a well-rehearsed tune, and a lot of nerve. Little by little he learned, however, and he worked often for Louis Thomas during the next couple of years.

As a journeyman piano player, Duke would take any job. One of the strangest was for a man who was part magician, part fortuneteller. Duke's job was to play background music to suit the mood the fortuneteller was trying to set. Duke recalled later that he was amazed at his own ability "to fall into the spirit of the very serious and sometimes mystic moods."

Duke had also begun "jamming" with saxophonist Otto Hardwick, trumpeter Arthur Whetsol, and banjo player Elmer Snowden. They would get together in a building called the True Reformers Hall and try to imitate the sounds of other local bands. The players didn't know it then, but they would become the nucleus of the first really professional Ellington band.

Duke was scheduled to graduate from high school in June 1917. He had been offered a scholarship to study art at the Pratt Institute of Applied Arts in Brooklyn, New York. It was a fine school, one of the country's best at the time. Two years earlier, Duke might have jumped at the chance. But now music had replaced art as his major interest. And music was beginning to bring in money. So instead of continuing in school, he decided to drop out and pursue music.

One night Louis Thomas sent him out on a one-man job playing under-conversation music at a fancy club. When Thomas said, *"Collect a hundred dollars and bring me ninety,"* Duke started thinking. He was being paid ten dollars for a night's work, while Thomas, who only booked the job, was getting ninety. Duke decided then and there to strike out on his own. The next day he took an ad in the telephone book that read:

MUSIC FOR ALL OCCASIONS

Then he began collecting his own musicians and sending them out on jobs. Soon Duke was sending out four or five bands a night, playing with one and collecting a fee for booking the others. He wasn't just a musician; he was also a shrewd businessman. In addition to his bands, he helped operate a sign-painting business. Sometimes he would paint the signs advertising a dance, then go and play at it with one of his bands. Within a year or two he had earned enough money to buy a house and a car—a great accomplishment for any young man of his age in 1918, and an amazing accomplishment for a young black man.

That year Duke took on still another job, working for the State Department as a daytime messenger. The State Department later transferred him to the Navy Transportation Division, where his job was to make all the train reservations for Navy officers. The United States was then fighting in World War I, and military travel was an important business. Duke learned the schedules of every train in the country. Years later, that knowledge would be useful to him.

In July 1918 Duke had married his high-school sweetheart, Edna Thompson. In 1919 their son, Mercer, was born. The couple soon separated. Duke devoted more and more time to his bands.

Before long, Duke was concentrating more on music and less on his business. He had a good head for business, but he wanted to play new things and learn more about the music he was playing. It would one day be known as jazz, and it would eventually gain world-wide popularity. But in 1919, the "new music" was just taking shape, growing from several different roots in black America.

3

The Birth of Jazz

When asked, late in his career, to define jazz, Duke Ellington said, "It is a music with an African foundation which came out of an American environment."

When he was born, the word *jazz* itself did not exist as a musical term. There was a new kind of music springing up in various parts of the country, but it was yet unnamed—nothing like it had ever been heard in America.

The black men who were creating this new music were born here—their families had been in this country for generations, originally brought as slaves. But the basic rhythms and distinctive harmonies of the music could be traced back to Africa, where the ancestors of these men lived.

Jazz historian Charles Edward Smith suggests that the slave owners in America made a point of forcing their slaves to give up their African languages and religions. But African music "was *not,* generally speaking, destroyed in America."

By 1900, almost three hundred years after the first slaves were brought to America, musicians in black communities in different parts of the country were still playing kinds of music that could be traced back to African roots. They had either borrowed or composed lyrics in English, and they had sometimes used melodies from European and white American sources. But there was always still a difference between their music and that of the whites.

European music was usually written down to be performed by orchestras or bands or soloists. By contrast, black music had an improvised quality. Different groups or soloists might use the same song, but no two groups would play or sing it quite the same. In fact, the same performer would likely do the song differently from one night to the next. In many ways skillful improvising is more difficult than playing or singing from a sheet of music. The musicians must know and understand the form and the harmonic structure of a piece in order to improvise at all. And when a group plays together, each musician must be tuned in to what the others are doing.

Another characteristic of the music in black communities was its steady, emphatic rhythm. There were worksongs, designed to be sung to the rhythm of hard physical labor, pulsating spirituals, and dancing songs for rejoicing. Even the sad songs—the blues and the slow, grieving spirituals—had a characteristic rhythmic strength that was quite different from the music inherited from Europe.

The first music from the black community to gain an audience among white people was ragtime piano. Ragtime grew up in the early 1890s, flourished for a little more than a decade, then slowly faded into the background as other forms began to take its place. It was the first black music to be recorded—by the new invention called the player piano. A ragtime pianist could have his music transferred to a roll of paper by a machine that put a hole in the paper for each note struck. When this roll was put in a special player piano—in a café or the living room of a home—the piece could be played back. The operator just pushed rhythmically on two pedals and the contraption played by means of air forced through the holes of the paper. Ragtime pieces were also sold as sheet music. The first "hit song" in America was a ragtime tune by Scott Joplin called "Maple Leaf Rag," of which 100,000 sheet-music copies were sold.

What is ragtime? To the ear it's a bouncing, happy music, with an even, walking bass (or lower) line, and a smart, generally fast-paced melody line. It was once described very simply as "music involving syncopation [accents on what are normally the weak beats of the measure] with the right hand, while the left hand plays a precise bass."

But rags were not simple, in either their composition or their execution. It took pianists of great skill to play them well. The composers often wove three or four different melodic lines into one piece. They were generally played as written without any spontaneous improvisation, and that's why later commentators did not consider them as jazz. But there is no doubt that ragtime did have great influence on the birth of jazz and that its influence was greatest on pianists. In fact, the popularity of ragtime probably assured that the piano would be an important jazz instrument.

The area of Sedalia, Missouri, is generally looked upon as the birthplace of ragtime piano music, although similar forms may have been developing in other sections of the country at about the same time. The black pianists in this small town in mid-Missouri—those who provided entertainment in the honky-tonks (bars), clubs, and bawdy houses—developed the new style of playing. At first, ragtime was considered low and vulgar by respectable blacks and whites. But its popularity grew and the ragtime style spread, first to St. Louis, then to the rest of the country.

There were many fine composers of ragtime. Among the best were Scott Joplin and Tom Turpin. (Joplin's music was used in the 1970s for an award-winning film, *The Sting,* and his opera *Treemonisha* was performed on Broadway.) White musicians soon began writing and playing rags, too. A dance called the *cakewalk* was invented to go along with the music, and the teen-agers at the turn of the century soon learned it. The cakewalk was the first of many dance crazes that would grow from the new music.

In the meantime, ragtime piano was changing. Ferdinand "Jelly Roll" Morton was one of the first to begin opening up the strict ragtime form. Morton's playing was freer. He varied the conventional ragtime bass line, and he also began improvising in the melody line.

After Morton's innovations came those of James P. Johnson, who was the most important man in the shift from ragtime piano to jazz piano. Johnson became known as a stride pianist because his left hand appeared to stride up and down the keyboard, producing a looser, more swinging rhythm than conventional ragtime. Because he was based in Harlem, a black section of New York City, his style became known as the Eastern, or Harlem, style. Critic Gunther Schuller has pointed out that the swinging rhythms Johnson added to ragtime piano seemed to come from the blues, a traditional form of black music.

The blues grew out of worksongs first sung by slaves in work gangs. Their words almost always tell a story of sweat and toil, of disappointment and unhappiness. A blues song has a strict form—twelve bars of four beats each—and a simple harmonic structure that uses only three chords. But within these limits there can be a great variation of mood and much spontaneous improvisation. Those who sang the blues knew how to use the form to catch their own mood or the mood of their audience at the moment they were performing. In many ways a blues tune was a different piece of music every time it was performed.

Many people believe that the blues developed only on the Southern plantations, where blacks sang in the fields and in work gangs. But after slavery was abolished, the blues was sung wherever there were black people at work. Willie "the Lion" Smith, a stride pianist who was to be a major influence on Duke Ellington, was a native of New York State, born in the town of Goshen in 1897. When asked where the blues came from, he replied, "Here's one that'll kill 'em. The blues comes from the brickyards in Haverstraw, New York, where those colored people worked in the brickyards. They sang blues all day."

So the blues was widespread, coming into existence wherever black people lived and worked. After 1900, black musicians took the blues form and feeling and combined it with other forms. James P. Johnson and

Willie Smith combined blues with ragtime piano, and soon others began to "sing" the blues on other instruments as well.

If jazz was "born" anywhere, it was born in New Orleans. That city, near the mouth of the Mississippi River, was a lively port town with a large black population. During the 1890s a new kind of band and a new kind of music began to emerge there.

The basic rhythms and melodies that came from Africa and developed on Southern plantations were familiar in New Orleans. But there the musical heritage was picked up, not by ragtime pianists or society dance bands, but by brass bands that played for every occasion from parades to funerals. The musicians in these bands began to experiment with different elements of the black musical heritage. In addition to marches and hymns, they played pensive, slow blues and lively stomps. At the same time, instead of sticking to preset arrangements, they let individual musicians improvise.

Soon a new kind of band became popular. It had a cornet, a trombone, a clarinet, and a rhythm section made up of a piano, a string bass or tuba, and drums. The piano was strictly a rhythm instrument in the New Orleans style of playing. The rhythm section was the cornerstone of the group, providing the beat. It was the rhythm section that gave the music its life, made it move and swing.

The cornet, a smaller version of the trumpet, usually carried the lead, or melody, while the trombone added a lower harmonic line, touching on the melody only from time to time. The clarinet often improvised in the upper register, providing a kind of descant—a second melody that complemented the main melody. Though trombone and clarinet parts were often improvised, these instruments didn't play true solos at first. And the cornet played only very short solos during "breaks"—the pauses between choruses. This new, freer form, the combination of three instruments playing different lines, gave the music its "polyphonic," or many-voiced, sound. The three horns rarely played the same melody line. Within a few years, this new style of music received the name *jazz*.

In 1915, while Duke Ellington was still in high school, Joe "King" Oliver and his band played their first engagement in New Orleans. Oliver was a cornetist of immense power and drive. Over the years, he developed a group that was free and improvisational yet disciplined.

In 1918 Oliver went to Chicago to play. Two years later, he organized King Oliver's Creole Jazz Band. In 1922, the band played at the Lincoln Gardens in Chicago with a new young second cornetist named Louis Armstrong. Within a few years, Armstrong became the first major soloist to break away from the strict New Orleans tradition of ensemble playing. By the time he died in 1971, he was known around the world for his exciting performances and his contributions to jazz.

New Orleans jazz was picked up by white musicians from the very beginning. The first jazz recordings were made in 1917 by a white band from New Orleans, the Original Dixieland Jazz Band. It was not as good a group as King Oliver's Creole Jazz Band, but the term *Dixieland* for this kind of music caught on. Years later, when there were many different kinds of jazz, the old Dixieland style had a great revival. Dixieland groups are still popular.

Black musicians in other parts of the country were also contributing to the new music. In Texas and Oklahoma, parade bands were common. They learned to swing in a way all their own and such bands contributed many fine musicians to the jazz world. The Midwest was a meeting place for music from the East, the South, and the Southwest. Clarinetist Garvin Bushell, from Springfield, Ohio, recalled the activity there: "Until about 1919 ragtime piano was the major influence in that section of the country," he said. "The change [to jazz] began to come around 1912 to 1915 when the four-string banjo and the saxophone came in. The players began to elaborate on the melodic lines; the harmony and rhythm remained the same."

The experiment with saxophones, which were used up to then only in marching and concert bands, was a great success. Soon the saxophone would become one of the instruments most closely identified with jazz.

When Bushell visited Chicago, he went to hear King Oliver's band. "It was the first time I'd heard New Orleans jazz to any advantage," he recalled, "and I studied them every night for the entire week we were in town. I was very impressed with their blues and their sound. . . . We sat there with our mouths open."

Bushell's reaction suggests how seriously musicians took the new music, and it also shows how musical ideas from different parts of the country spread as bands and listeners moved around more freely. Bushell said that the sound of Oliver's band was "less cultivated" than the Eastern sound he was familiar with, but he felt the New Orleans sound "touched you more" and was "more expressive of how people felt."

Duke Ellington must have heard a New Orleans band about the same time as Bushell, and he must have been as excited and shocked at the harsher "gutbucket" sounds. How could the new music keep the expressiveness of the New Orleans bands, yet be as elegant and subtle as that of the best musicians in the East? This was one of the major questions Ellington would be trying to solve in the coming years. The elements of many different musical traditions were coming together—African rhythms, black people's worksongs and spirituals, the blues, ragtime piano, brass bands. Duke Ellington was about to enter this fluid and exciting musical world.

4

The Washingtonians

By 1919, Duke's business was flourishing. He was playing with his own band, was a booking agent for his other bands, and continued as a sign painter. He was still a long way from being a musical innovator. Yet Duke was earning about $150 a week—equal to $500 or $600 a week today. For a black man just barely twenty years old and living in a racially segregated city, he was a huge success.

Then one day at the house of a friend, Percy Johnson, Duke heard a new piano roll made by James P. Johnson (no relation to Percy). Duke sat spellbound as the player piano produced the sounds of "Carolina Shout." He recalled years later the impression James P.'s new stride style had on him: "This was . . . an entirely new avenue of adventure for me and I went back there every day and listened. Percy slowed the mechanism down so that I could see which keys on the piano were going down as I digested Johnson's wonderful sounds. I played with it until I had his 'Carolina Shout' down pat."

Soon he was playing the Johnson masterpiece at rent parties. Then one day the great James P. himself came to Washington. He was playing at Convention Hall and Duke and his friends were in the audience. After Johnson played "Carolina Shout" Duke's friends began pushing Duke up toward the stage, shouting that he could play the piece as well as the master. James P. stepped aside to let the youngster play. Duke was scared stiff, but when he finished everyone applauded, including Johnson.

"I didn't play any more that night," Duke said in his autobiography, "but just leaned over the piano and listened to the one and only. What I absorbed on that occasion might, I think, have constituted a whole semester in a conservatory. Afterward, he [James P.] elected me his guide for a tour of all the Washington joints, and I stayed up until 10 A.M."

Much of the music Ellington played in public in those early days was "commercial"—not really jazz at all. Like most black musicians in the East, he copied the sounds of the white society bands, showy groups that worked for white audiences. They played mostly music for dancing—waltzes, ballads, fox trots, and an occasional ragtime tune. Duke and the bands he sent out played before many white audiences. And both whites and middle-class blacks preferred the respectable music of the time to jazz, which was still thought to be vulgar and low. Ellington would become a jazz musician only gradually, adding elements of the new music over a period of years.

Duke learned the white-oriented musical forms and stuck with them even after he was recognized as a top jazz musician. The thirty-two-bar song form, for example, presented more possibilities for variations in style than the twelve-bar blues form. And he drew ideas from other kinds of musical groups. The thirty- or forty-piece bands that played in the movie palaces were by no means jazz bands. They performed before, during, and after the silent movies, playing all kinds of musical works from classical pieces to contemporary marches, with some jazz-oriented tunes mixed in. Duke was fascinated by the complex arrangements that these bands used. He got ideas of his own from listening, and he talked to the bands' arrangers and leaders whenever he could. He was already aware that a band's style could be important, too, and the best theater bands appealed to him because they were well dressed and well rehearsed.

The early years of the 1920s were good times in Washington and other big cities. The decade became known as "the Jazz Age" because during those years the new music had its first great burst of popularity. Most people associated jazz with the new nightspots where they could get together and drink illegal liquor.

In 1920 a new amendment to the Constitution made it illegal to make or sell alcoholic beverages. The intention of this "Prohibition" law was to abolish the evils of alcohol by making it impossible to get. But during the Prohibition era, which lasted until 1933, people seemed to drink more, not less. A new illegal industry, called bootlegging, grew up. Bootleggers made and sold liquor although it was against the law.

So despite Prohibition, most clubs still served liquor, and many people had it in their homes. Underground bars, called speak-easies, were soon in operation everywhere. Because there were so many places to buy and drink liquor, the police in many cities soon gave up trying to stop the illegal traffic.

Meanwhile, the clubs and speak-easies became the home of the new music, a place where musicians could sit all night trying out their new ideas. The audiences were appreciative, and the pay was good, thanks to the high profit on illegal and untaxed liquor.

Although there was some excitement in the Washington jazz scene, Duke and his friends soon began looking to bigger things and places. In 1919 the Duke had met a showy young drummer named Sonny Greer, who was playing for a theater orchestra in Washington. Greer was a flashy musician. But more important, according to Duke, "he had been to New York, and anybody who had been to New York had the edge on us." Greer talked as well as he played—and he was immensely impressed with Ellington. He soon joined the Ellington band. He filled the heads of the band members with dreams and images of the exciting New York scene. Before long Duke himself was eager to leave Washington, even if it meant giving up his lucrative band-booking and sign-painting businesses.

Then, in 1922, the opportunity came. A bandleader named Wilbur Sweatman wanted Sonny Greer to join him in the big city. Sonny said he'd go, but he was already stubbornly loyal to his new friends. He insisted that Otto Hardwick, Arthur Whetsol, Elmer Snowden, and Duke come with him. Sweatman said he'd try to find a spot for all five, but he found jobs only for Duke, Sonny, and Hardwick. The other two had to scout for jobs on their own.

Wilbur Sweatman is best remembered as a man who could play three clarinets at the same time, a juggling feat of no small means. His band was only on the fringes of the jazz world, playing mostly in vaudeville theaters. A vaudeville show was a large live variety show. There were singers and dancers, comedians, jugglers, acrobats, and animal acts. Performers came on one after another in rapid succession. A band such as Sweatman's accompanied all these acts and played a bit on its own before and after the show and during the breaks. There was money on the vaudeville circuit then, and Sweatman concentrated on making it. Duke said he learned something about show business from Sweatman, but he didn't gain much musical satisfaction.

Unfortunately, the boys from Washington had come at a bad time. In a matter of weeks Sweatman's bookings suddenly dwindled, and Duke and the other two were out of jobs. Now all five were without work. Life for Duke and his friends became one big hustle.

"[Sonny Greer] and I hustled around playing pool," he wrote. "We might start with a quarter. The minute we got two dollars, we'd quit, go home, dress up, order two steak dinners, give the girl a quarter, and have a quarter left for tomorrow. We'd be pretty, clean, and neat, and we'd go cabareting, visit Willie 'the Lion' Smith, or James P. Johnson, or Fats Waller. . . .

"We would never send home for money because we knew that would scare our people to death, [and] stories about our splitting a hot dog five ways were more of a gag than anything else. We were getting more bored with our situation than desperate, until one day I had the luck to find fifteen dollars on the street. Then we had a square meal, got on the train, and went back to Washington to get ourselves together before we tried it again."

Their second chance came about a year later. In the spring of 1923 Duke and his friends learned of an engagement in New York. Greer and Hardwick went first.

Duke followed a few days later. Since he expected a job to be waiting, he traveled to New York in style, spending all his money on the way. But when he arrived the first thing Sonny asked for was money.

"Hey, Duke, buddy, give us something," the drummer said. "We're all busted and waiting for you to relieve the situation."

"Sorry, I'm broke, too," Duke answered. "I blew it all on the trip up from Washington."

The engagement the band had come for was no longer available. Once again the group was in New York with no job, few prospects . . . and no money. But this time there was help. The generous Willie "the Lion" Smith let the boys sit in with him and split the tips. So did guitarist Freddy Guy. They were just scraping by, gigging around, waiting for a solid job to open up.

Whenever Duke came to a crossroads in his life, someone always seemed to appear to show him the way. This time the person was Ada "Bricktop" Smith, a singer whose nickname came from a shock of very red hair. Bricktop felt sorry for the boys and spoke with Barron Wilkins, owner of a club in Harlem appropriately called Barron's.

Harlem was New York's largest black neighborhood, uptown from the business and theater districts. At that time Harlem itself was a major entertainment center for audiences of all races. Barron's was a place where successful black people such as comedian Bert Williams and former heavyweight boxing champ Jack Johnson often went. Popular white entertainers such as Al Jolson also came regularly. And thanks to the persuasive powers of Ada Smith, the new house band consisted of Duke

Ellington, Sonny Greer, Arthur Whetsol, Otto Hardwick, and Elmer Snowden. They called themselves the Washingtonians.

Duke's music at Barron's was good, but nothing sensational or really different. The band played society music from Washington, numbers that came out of their many jam sessions, and works picked up from other groups. The instrumentation was simple—Ellington on piano, Snowden on banjo, Greer on drums, Whetsol on trumpet, and Hardwick on C-melody saxophone—so there was no need for any kind of real arrangements. The Washingtonians may have experimented with elements of the blues and the new sounds from New Orleans, but they played mostly "straight."

Duke himself had begun to imitate the striding techniques of James P. Johnson and Willie "the Lion" Smith, bringing him closer to real jazz piano. He listened to them as often as possible, and both musicians were always happy to help him. There was a camaraderie among musicians in those days. They seemed to sense that they were all part of the same struggle, giving birth to a new kind of music.

In a matter of weeks the Washingtonians gained a huge following at Barron's. It wasn't only their music; it was their sense of showmanship, their appearance, their attitude. The band was always very conscious of its appearance, the dapper Arthur Whetsol leading the way. "If any one of us came in dressed improperly," Duke wrote, "Whetsol would flick his cigarette ash in a certain way, or pull down the lower lid of his right eye with his forefinger and stare at the offending party."

By the autumn of 1923, the band had become well

known. Many prominent show people came to Barron's, and everyone liked the friendly and talented Washingtonians. Soon they received other offers, and before the end of the year they moved downtown to the Hollywood Club, which was later renamed the Kentucky Club. That would be their home for the next four years.

Until the band moved to the Kentucky Club, Elmer Snowden had been its leader. Duke never really wanted the job. He was satisfied playing the piano and trying his hand as a songwriter. Snowden seemed to have the best business sense of the five anyway.

However, it was business matters that eventually caused a rift between Elmer and the others. Snowden decided to leave and was replaced by Freddy Guy on banjo and guitar. Duke took over as leader almost by default. The band was small and didn't require much leadership at first, and Duke just served as its spokesman.

The owner of the Kentucky Club, a dapper little white man named Leo Bernstein, took a liking to the Washingtonians right from the start. He respected them as musicians and genuinely liked them as individuals. He was always fair in his dealings with them. And business was always good.

There were classy patrons at the Kentucky. Socialites and show-business folk mixed freely, drinking homemade Prohibition booze and listening to the Washingtonians. Al Jolson and Jimmy Durante were two well-known white entertainers who made the Kentucky their regular hangout. Even the gangsters who helped supply the liquor spent time in the club. They were shady characters with a reputation for violence, but like everyone else, they liked the music—and most of them were big tippers. Between their regular income and the tips, the musicians did very well.

"We might leave the club with a hundred dollars each in our pockets," Duke recalled, "but by the time we got home we would have blown it all, because we had to go from joint to joint to be received, and to find out what was happening."

There were always breakfast dances up in Harlem in those days, and on many nights the band couldn't wait to finish at the Kentucky so they could hustle uptown and join the party.

The Prohibition laws posed only a slight problem. The Kentucky Club, like all the others, served liquor to its paying customers. There was just one worry. How would waiters be able to tell when a supposed customer was really a "plant," a federal agent checking to see if liquor was being sold?

The answer to this problem came from Sonny Greer. "Let me take care of this," he said. "I'll give the word on who gets the drinks and who doesn't." Whenever a customer asked for a drink, the waiter would look to the bandstand. Sonny would size up the situation in an instant, then nod either yes or no. No one knew how Sonny could tell the difference between a real customer and a plant, but the story is that he never made a mistake. There were no raids at the Kentucky Club while the Ellington band, with Sonny Greer, was playing there.

The celebrities continued to come. Paul Whiteman became a regular visitor. "Pops," as he was called, was the leader of the most popular dance orchestra in the

country. Whiteman took an interest in the new sounds
and rhythms that were being brought to the city by black
musicians. During 1923, the Whiteman Orchestra gave
the first performance of George Gershwin's *Rhapsody in
Blue*. Gershwin, a white composer, had used new jazz
rhythms in his piece and Whiteman was given credit for
taking the *Rhapsody* into the concert hall and "making a
lady out of jazz."

Whether or not *Rhapsody in Blue* and the orchestra-
tions of Paul Whiteman were really jazz is still a matter
of opinion. But it is important that Whiteman and other
white musicians were interested in jazz because they
helped to bring the new music to a huge new audience.

During the Kentucky Club period, from 1923 to 1927,
the Washingtonians began changing from a society, or
dance, band to a jazz band. And once the change began,
it continued at an increasing pace on several different
levels.

To begin with, new musicians—additions to the
band—brought new musical ideas and new sounds.
Trombonist Charlie Irvis sometimes covered the bell of
his horn with a smashed tomato can, using it as a mute.
This gave his horn a rough, growling sound. Because of
the mute, his nickname was Charlie "Plug." The reaction to Irvis's playing was mixed, among both band and
audience. He'd go down to the low register of his horn
and growl at the customers, making humanlike grunts
and groans. Charlie Plug left the band before his playing
could be judged on an artistic level, but his sound—called
"jungle-istic" by Ellington—made the band unique

The entrance to Barron's Cabaret in Harlem, early 1920s.

The first Cotton Club band, 1927. Left to right: Duke Ellington, piano; *Joe "Tricky Sam" Nanton*, trombone; *Sonny Greer*, drums; *Bubber Miley*, trumpet; *Harry Carney*, baritone sax; *Wellman Braud*, bass; *Rudy Jackson, Nelson Kincaid*, reeds; *Freddy Guy*, banjo/guitar; *Ellsworth Reynolds*, violin.

Duke Ellington and his Orchestra, 1931. Seated, left to right: Freddy Jenkins, Cootie Williams, Arthur Whetsol, trumpets; Harry Carney, Johnny Hodges, Barney Bigard, reeds. Standing, left to right: Joe Nanton, trombone; unidentified trombonist; Sonny Greer, drums; Duke Ellington, conductor/piano; Freddy Guy, banjo; Wellman Braud, bass.

among those groups playing at clubs like the Kentucky. And his growling served to open Duke's eyes to the playing of Bubber Miley.

In late 1924 Arthur Whetsol told Duke he was leaving to attend medical school. The logical thing would have been to find another sweet-sounding trumpet player like Whetsol. Instead, Duke and his men found James "Bubber" Miley.

Like Irvis, Miley was New York–born with a very casual attitude toward life. He grew up in a rough section of the city and knew how to work hard and play hard. And he could do wonders with his horn. Like Irvis, he loved to make his horn growl, and he used a rubber plunger—the kind a plumber uses to clear a drain—as a mute. It was placed over the regular mute and had to be deftly maneuvered with the left hand, not an easy thing to do.

Miley's music represented something new—something heard before this time only in back rooms and basements. As clarinetist Garvin Bushell recalled, when talking about the New York scene in the early 1920s, "You could only hear the blues and real jazz in the gutbucket cabarets where the lower class went. You usually weren't allowed to play blues . . . in the average Negro middle-class home. That music supposedly suggested a low element."

But that's what Bubber played. Duke himself said, "Bubber used to growl all night long, playing gutbucket on his horn. That was when we decided to forget all about the sweet music."

Duke didn't tamper with Miley's sound, and soon Bubber's playing attracted a whole new following for the band. Other musicians came to listen and some even

came to jam with the Washingtonians. New Orleans–
born Sidney Bechet was one. He played clarinet and
soprano saxophone, and loved to jam with Miley, pitting
his New Orleans background against Miley's New York
style. It made great music and, for an acute listener like
Duke, presented a wealth of new ideas.

Critic and jazz historian Stanley Dance, who collaborated with Duke on his autobiography, said, "The en-
counter with Bubber Miley was of great significance
because this is the man with the plunger mute. I think
the idea of the wa-wa mute making animal and childish
noises was probably fairly common. But Bubber Miley
turned it into a jungle-sounding thing with much more
dramatic force and color. It was almost a humorous
device before, but with Miley you were forced to take it
seriously."

Soon after Miley joined the band, Charlie Irvis left and
was replaced by Joe Nanton. Nanton was quickly nicknamed "Tricky Sam" by Hardwick because "he could
always do with one hand what someone else did with
two." Nanton took over the growl-trombone role and he
and Miley went to work with their plungers, making the
Ellington band the most talked-about group in New York.

Nanton and Miley played beautifully together. And
Duke let them develop their sound without a complaint.
Their intensely personal kind of playing found a permanent place in the Ellington band, helping to shift the
group toward jazz and influencing Ellington himself for
years to come. With his two plunger men he saw possibilities for new sounds and new combinations of sounds.
For a while he just let the men go and listened.

But even while he was listening and learning, Duke

began trying his hand as a composer. He hadn't been in New York long when he learned that anybody could take songs to the many music publishers located on Broadway. A music-publisher's office was always a wild scene—six, eight, ten pianos crowded into a small room with aspiring composers banging away on all of them, trying to impress the publisher with their latest creations. Duke joined the action with his usual enthusiasm.

He worked with a lyricist named Joe Trent, and the two began trying to sell their quickie compositions. At first they met with no success at all. Finally they hit with one, a sale that brought a fifty-dollar advance against future royalties (money earned if the sheet music sold well enough). The year was 1923 and the song was called "Blind Man's Buff."

The two men thought they had found the formula. However, as Duke said later, "I had broken the ice and at the same time gotten hooked on writing music. [But] the next day, and for many to follow, we were back in our old rut—peddling songs and failing to find any buyers."

Music publishing was a frantic business. One day in 1924, Joe Trent came running up to Duke on the street. "We've got an offer, maybe a good one," he shouted. "We've got to write a show."

"When?" asked Duke, casually.

"Tonight," screamed the excited Trent. "We've got to do it tonight!"

Not one to turn his back on a $500 advance, Duke agreed. He and Trent went to work, Duke at the piano on one side of the room, Trent at a desk on the other side. The notes came in clusters; so did the words. By the next day the show was finished. It was called *Chocolate*

Kiddies, and though it never reached Broadway, its producer, Jack Robbins, took it to Germany, where it ran for two years at the Berlin Wintergarten. A show score in one night? Why not! Duke could always work when the deadlines were tight.

Just about the time Duke began composing regularly, he met Irving Mills, who was to become the band's booking agent and manager, as well as Duke's business partner. Mills first saw the band at the Kentucky Club, and apparently he saw their promise. Finally he approached Duke and said he'd like to record some of his music. Duke jumped at the chance, and he and Mills worked together for fifteen years.

Recording was still in its infancy. Unlike today's stereophonic records, which are made with a multitude of electronic devices and microphones, records in the 1920s were crude and chancy. There was just one primitive microphone for the entire band. And the record itself was a crude disk with giant grooves. The music was picked up by a heavy needle—along with lots of hissing background noise. The resulting sound was hollow and empty, and it was almost impossible to achieve an authentic reproduction. So Duke learned to experiment with sounds. If the band played exactly the same way for a recording as it did at the Kentucky Club, the recording sound might be terrible. Duke worked on new combinations of instruments that might not work in a live performance, but produced the best effect on a recording. He became one of the first expert recording musicians, learning to use the new medium in new ways.

The early records were limited to three minutes on a side, which put pressure on a composer to keep his pieces short. To the Duke, this was just one more challenge to overcome, and he soon learned to use this limitation to his advantage. Years later, pianist Billy Taylor said, "Duke was a master of the short, concise musical statement. . . . He really would organize those things so they were close to perfect. Some of them were masterpieces and they were under three minutes long."

Irving Mills got the band plenty of chances to record. In fact, once they started, the recordings came at a fast and furious pace. Mills would often grab Duke right after the band had finished for the night and say, "Have four numbers ready for recording at nine o'clock tomorrow morning."

Mills was a good manager with a very smart way of doing things. To get as many recording dates as possible he went to many different companies, and gave the band a different name at each place. They recorded as Duke Ellington on the Victor label, the Jungle Band on Brunswick, the Washingtonians on Harmony, the Whoopee Makers on Perfect, Sonny Greer and His Memphis Men on Columbia, the Harlem Footwarmers on Okeh, and even more.

Some of the very first records were uneven. The recording quality was poor and the band had often had too little time for rehearsal. As critic Gunther Schuller wrote of one of these sides, "Duke's piano was at the time a very sloppy, helter-skelter sort of party piano, and he and certain other members of the band had a tendency to rush tempos." But there was also much to admire—especially some of the early solos by Bubber Miley.

Duke was still feeling his way as a composer. But he seemed to know already that Bubber Miley was his most interesting and most innovative soloist. In the early recordings Duke's objective was to provide a framework to show Miley at his best. A good example is "Rainy Nights," made in 1926.

At the beginning of the number the melody is played by Otto Hardwick on alto sax, a catchy but straight tune with few frills, backed up by a careful, even beat. In the New Orleans style, each of the four beats in a measure gets an accent. The same rhythmic feeling continues through a trombone solo by Charlie Irvis. Then Miley comes in and everything changes. Duke abandons the four-four rhythm and the band begins to "swing." The whole piece comes alive, and Miley's trumpet work makes the recording much more than an ordinary tune. The listener realizes the Washingtonians are on the brink of something very new and special.

In November 1926, the band recorded a tune called "East St. Louis Toodle-oo," and it's generally recognized as Ellington's first recorded masterpiece. It got such a good reception that it was Duke's theme song for a number of years afterward. Miley and trombonist Tricky Sam Nanton are the star soloists. As with many Ellington tunes, "East St. Louis Toodle-oo" sought to paint a picture. "The title meant, for me," Duke told Stanley Dance, "the broken walk of a man who had worked all day in the sun and was leaving the field at sunset. I had never been in East St. Louis then, but I thought the locale sounded right."

On this recording, as with so many others, the sounds produced by Miley's horn are almost like words. In fact, they often came directly from words. Anything Bubber saw or heard he'd try to reproduce on his horn, many

times with startling results. Though a seemingly care-
free man, Miley would spend hours working on combinations of sounds that he could incorporate into solos.

The recordings of the 1920s are poor in quality. But
they are important because they have preserved the
music of Duke Ellington and dozens of other early jazz
musicians. Without them, the world of the new music in
the 1920s would be hazy and hard to imagine, and
Ellington's development as a musician would be almost
impossible to trace. The notes of Bubber Miley's solos and
the Duke's arrangements could be written down on paper. But no one would ever be sure what Miley and the
Washingtonians really sounded like without hearing
their records, because jazz is such a personal kind of
expression. So jazz and Duke Ellington depended on the
invention of recorded sound to make their mark on the
world.

5

The Cotton Club

In the autumn of 1927, luck stepped into Duke Ellington's life once again. The band had recently left the Kentucky Club and was playing one-nighters and week-long engagements at theaters around the East. For the first time in several years, the band's future was hazy.

At the same time, the prestigious Cotton Club in Harlem was looking for a new house band. The previous band had played the New Orleans/Chicago style of jazz made famous by King Oliver's Creole Jazz Band. Now the Cotton Club tried to get King Oliver himself. But the King played hard to get. He turned down the club's first offer for a long-term run.

Irving Mills learned about the opening at the Cotton Club and began pushing for Duke. The club wanted a band of ten or eleven pieces. So to audition for the job, Duke had to add a couple of local musicians in a hurry. In a way, it was a risky venture. The band had grown very close, both musically and personally. Now Duke was faced with the prospect of enlarging the band, and in effect, changing it. Sonny Greer recalled his reaction, in *The World of Duke Ellington:* "That was one of the few times in my life that I wanted to leave the band. We were established and we were doing so well, but the pressure

went on and we had to go up there [to the Cotton Club].
We had to enlarge the band, too, and that broke my heart,
because everything had been so quiet and tasteful."

But Duke went ahead and auditioned. Luckily the band
was one of the last to audition. The boss of the Cotton
Club got there just in time to hear it, and he must have
liked what he heard. As Duke said, it was "a classic
example of being at the right place at the right time with
the right thing before the right people."

The band was playing for a vaudeville show at a
theater in Philadelphia when Duke learned the Cotton
Club job was his. The contract called for the band to open
in New York on December 4, 1927. But Ellington had
agreed to play in Philadelphia through December 11, and
the theater manager wouldn't let him break the agree-
ment.

According to one account, the manager of the theater
in Philadelphia had a visit from some tough characters
who suggested he change his mind and let the Ellington
band go early. The men may have been mobsters who
supplied liquor to the Cotton Club and wanted to make
sure that Duke got to his big new engagement on time.
Whatever the reason, Duke did open at the Cotton Club
on December 4, as advertised.

Although it was located in Harlem, the Cotton Club
catered primarily to a white audience. Famous or wealthy
blacks could get in, but the common people living in the
area were rarely seen inside. They didn't have the money.

The club was a former dance hall on the second floor of
a building and seated 400 people, but the band was not
the primary attraction. Scores of dancers, singers, and
other entertainers put on a lavish floor show, and the

band was there to provide musical support. A strong element of show biz dominated the atmosphere.

Duke recalled the place fondly. "The Cotton Club was a classy spot," he wrote. "Impeccable behavior was demanded in the room while the show was on. . . . The performers were paid high salaries, and the prices for the customers were high, too. They had about twelve dancing girls and eight show girls, and they were all beautiful chicks. They used to dress so well! On Sunday nights, when celebrities filled the joint, [the girls] would rush out of the dressing room after the show in all their finery. Every time they went by, the stars and the rich people would be saying, 'My, who is *that*?' "

At first the Duke and his band had a lot to learn. "The band went into the Cotton Club with a limited understanding of the big-time show world," wrote Barry Ulanov in his biography of Ellington. "Duke was not a leader in the sense that [other bandleaders of the day were]; on his feet or at the piano, he wasn't that kind of a showman. He wasn't a fast-talking master of ceremonies or a slick baton-waver; he didn't wear a battered hat or boast of playing more notes per minute than any other pianist. Nobody in the band wore funny hats and nobody clowned."

Duke learned quickly, however. The new emphasis on showmanship seemed to come naturally to him. Though he never became a clown or a showboat, he soon brought his own brand of class to the Cotton Club. He became acutely aware of the band's dress and appearance, and came up with various screening devices that made the band appear to be in shadows. His own stage presence also grew as he introduced the various acts, his own numbers, and the members of the band.

Duke had a keen eye for detail. Freddy Jenkins, a trumpeter who joined the band at the Cotton Club in 1928, had suffered a hand injury as a youngster that resulted in the loss of the fingertips on his right hand, the hand he used to finger the valves on his trumpet. Shortly after joining Duke, Jenkins started playing his horn left-handed.

"With Duke, you were in show business," said Jenkins, "and show business meant just that. You're there to perform, and nothing must interfere with the enjoyment of your patrons. You must try to hide any deformity you have which might divert their attention from what you are doing. You don't want them feeling sorry for you. You want them to enjoy the music."

Drummer Sonny Greer remembered another aspect of the band's new showmanship. "I was a drum designer for the Leedy Manufacturing Company of Elkhart, Indiana," he said, "and the president of the company had a fabulous set of drums made for me, with timpani, chimes, vibraphone, everything. Musicians used to come to the Cotton Club just to see it. The value of it was three thousand dollars, a lot of money at that time. . . . And I had Duke's name and my monogram on the front of it. I was the first in the world to do that."

"I saw many of the top bands of the day," recalled pianist Billy Taylor many years afterward. "Duke's was just so elegant, both musically and otherwise. . . . His band was always presented on a very high musical level, but also on a very high visual level. The lights were special, they would have a scrim [which produced the shadow effect], and would do several other pleasing visual things. It was a very good show, aside from the music they presented."

In the months after arriving at the Cotton Club, Duke also stabilized the band, permanently increasing it to twelve members. By late 1928, Bubber Miley had been joined on cornet by Freddy Jenkins and Arthur Whetsol, who had returned from a stint in medical school. Whetsol's pretty style of playing was a perfect contrast to Miley's growl. Trombonist Tricky Sam Nanton was joined by valve trombonist Juan Tizol, an outstanding group and section musician. Otto Hardwick had left to form his own band in 1928, but the reed section was still in fine hands. Johnny Hodges was now playing alto sax, New Orleans–born Barney Bigard doubled on tenor sax and clarinet, and young Harry Carney, at age seventeen, joined on baritone saxophone, becoming one of the first to use the big sax as a solo instrument in a jazz band. The rhythm section included Duke, Sonny Greer on drums, Freddy Guy on guitar, and Wellman Braud on bass.

Saxophonist Hodges deserves special mention. Except for a brief period in the early 1950s, he was to remain with the band for more than forty years, right up until his death in 1970. During that period, Hodges became a major voice in the band, its most popular soloist and highest-paid performer. His playing was a major influence on future generations of saxophone players. Though born in Boston, Hodges had been strongly influenced by New Orleans clarinetist/soprano saxophonist Sidney Bechet. Hodges combined elements of the Eastern and New Orleans styles in his playing. He had a bell-like, clear tone, which he used to weave beautiful, classical solos on ballads and slow lyrical numbers. But he could also swing on up-tempo and blues selections. Soon there wasn't an Ellington concert that didn't feature Johnny Hodges on several showcase numbers.

Duke now had a versatile and talented band to work with. Trumpeter Whetsol and saxophonist Hodges could handle the lyrical, pretty melodies, the ballads. And then there were Miley and Tricky Sam to take over with their plunger mutes on the compositions that called for a more elemental sound. It was perhaps this contrast of styles that gave the band its unique sound. Duke never tried to change a musician's style. His genius was his ability to use different styles and blend different sounds, working with each player and writing music for him as an individual. Duke didn't require that every musician be able to do everything, just that he make use of all his talents. In fact, Duke once said that if a man could play seven good notes, his job was to learn to get the most from those seven notes, and no more.

As the band got accustomed to the Cotton Club and came together as a unit, its music soon made the patrons forget their preference for the New Orleans and Chicago sounds. Jazz historians mark Ellington's arrival at the Cotton Club as the beginning of a new era in jazz.

Nothing stays unchanged for long, however. In 1928 and early 1929, Bubber Miley's health began to fail and he was finally forced to leave the band. (Miley never fully recovered and died in 1932.) He had made a sizable contribution to the band, and replacing him seemed almost impossible. But Duke's luck held. He discovered a young trumpeter named Cootie Williams playing with

Chick Webb's band and persuaded him to come up to the Cotton Club. Williams was a perfectionist and a powerful, innovative musician. But it took him a while to adjust to the new band, as he recalls in *The World of Duke Ellington:* "Duke never asked me to play like Bubber. Night after night I sat up there and nobody said a word. When Tricky Sam played [using the mute with his trombone] I laughed because it was funny. Funny-sounding to me. But it dawned on me, finally. I thought, 'This man hired me to take Bubber's place. And Bubber played with the plunger—like Tricky Sam.'

"For me it wasn't hard, learning to use the plunger. I'd never in my life thought to play like that, so it seemed funny at first. After I'd been doing it awhile, though, it became me. Or I became it—although I always played open [without a mute] as well.

"Those were my two ways of being. My plunger style was not like Bubber's. His soul wasn't my soul—and vice versa."

During the Cotton Club engagement a great change was taking place in Duke's career. He became more of a leader in public, acting as spokesman and master of ceremonies. And he also became more of a leader musically. When there had been only six men in the band, most of the music was unwritten. The band members talked over their approach to a tune, then they just played. Now, with twelve men and a whole show to put on, it was necessary for the band to have many more written arrangements. That job fell primarily to the Duke. He began to do serious arranging, considering the combination of instruments, and the various tonal and harmonic possibilities within his grasp.

At the same time, Irving Mills kept lining up one record date after another. From December 1927 to February 1931, while the band was at the Cotton Club, it participated in some sixty-four recording sessions, issuing more than 150 titles for many different companies. Duke wrote many of the tunes himself and did most of his own arranging.

In addition to his nightly chores at the Cotton Club and the increasing number of recording dates, Duke was spreading himself out in other ways. On days off the band would play area theaters, reaching new audiences. And under Mills's guidance, they took advantage of another new electronic invention: radio.

The first radio broadcast had taken place in 1916. Soon there were hundreds of stations across the country, and millions of people had radios in their homes. By 1924 it was possible to broadcast coast to coast. Irving Mills saw the potential of the new medium, and in 1928 Duke made his first nationwide broadcast from the Cotton Club. Radio introduced Ellington's music to people in many parts of the country.

Duke was also developing a distinctive style—so distinctive, in fact, that new band members had trouble adjusting. Barney Bigard, an outstanding clarinetist in the New Orleans tradition, had joined in 1927. "Just after I joined Duke," he wrote, "I used to think everything was wrong because he wrote so weird. It took me some time to get used to hearing all those things. He would make the chords all the wrong way, giving someone else the part he should have given the clarinet player."

Trumpeter Freddy Jenkins recalled how Duke arrived at some of those "weird" sounds: "He used to set us on the stand and pay us union scale, maybe for five hours, just to help him formulate chords. He'd assign different notes to every instrument in the band and say—'Play that, B-a-a-m!'—and it might produce a big C-13th, what we call a Christmas chord. Then he'd take those same notes and switch them to different instruments and while you'd still have a big C-13th, it would sure sound a lot different. Sometimes he'd do that three or four times before he found what he wanted."

The working routine was much more precise than the players were used to, but it was producing new sounds and giving Duke rich material for his arrangements, which were growing more complex and subtle.

Duke's experiments can be traced in the recordings he made during these years. Although the band improved and recording techniques were improving too, the big change was in the arrangements. Duke's first recordings depended on the solo ability of Bubber Miley and his plunger mute. During the Cotton Club years, Miley, and later Cootie Williams, continued to play the plunger-muted trumpet beautifully and artistically, but their role was not so prominent. The band as a whole and other soloists were being heard more and more.

The earliest important pieces were "Black and Tan Fantasy" and "Creole Love Call." The first looked backward, featuring two strong Miley solos. But the second was an experimental piece. Duke used a singer named Adelaide Hall to supply a wordless vocal to the arrangement, the first time that had been done on record. In effect, he was adding another instrument to the band.

Many of Duke's basic compositions were written quickly. (It's said that "Black and Tan Fantasy," for example, was written in a taxi as Duke headed toward a recording session.) But there was always time to refine them. The band recorded so often that Duke had the chance to produce several versions of the same tune, revising the arrangements and rehearsing the band ahead of time.

"The Mooch" is another outstanding early side, also featuring a wordless vocal, this time by Baby Cox. In early 1929, Duke recorded a tune called "Awful Sad," which was still another milestone for him. It was the first Ellington ballad that featured the gentle, lyrical trumpet of Arthur Whetsol. Up to then, the growling plunger trumpet had dominated. But Duke loved Whetsol's playing. Ballads weren't usually considered part of a jazz band's repertoire, but Duke played them, often featuring Arthur Whetsol.

Whetsol was called upon again for the 1930 recording of "Mood Indigo," another beautifully lyrical ballad which became Duke's first major songwriting hit. At first the melody is carried by Whetsol, with Barney Bigard on clarinet, and Joe Nanton on trombone providing the harmony. Later a sweet solo by Whetsol is contrasted with a more earthy solo by Bigard.

The combination of trumpet, clarinet, and trombone had been common from the earliest days of New Orleans jazz. But Duke's use of the trio in a ballad was revolutionary. And by writing close-pitched harmonies between the three, he produced a "mike-tone" that sounds almost like a fourth instrument. Ellington had developed what Gunther Schuller called "a totally new concept of sound."

One other important composition among the many of the period was "Creole Rhapsody," first recorded in 1929. It breaks completely with all previous conventions in

jazz composing and recording. In its earliest version it
was nearly twice as long as a conventional tune, two
sides of a ten-inch, 78-rpm record. A later version extended to both sides of a twelve-inch 78. Duke had
freed himself from the three-minute record side. "Creole
Rhapsody" combines arranged sectional and ensemble
work with solos by Duke himself, Cootie Williams on trumpet, Bigard on clarinet, Hodges on alto, and Harry Carney
on baritone sax.

Not everyone liked the "Creole Rhapsody," but critics
agreed that it was a bold experiment. The Duke would
experiment with even longer compositions in later years.
The one complaint heard most often was that Ellington
was turning away from improvisation by writing out the
parts almost as fully as a classical composer would.
Gunther Schuller said these compositions made the players "uncomfortable and rigid."

As Duke grew as an arranger and composer, he did
begin to impose more rigid patterns on his soloists. But
his arrangements usually brought out the creativity of
each of his soloists, so the band stuck together and
learned to live with his experiments.

The late 1920s were an exciting time not only at the
Cotton Club but in the rest of Harlem as well. The Duke
wrote years later, "Sometimes I wonder what my music
would sound like . . . had I not been exposed to the
sounds and over-all climate created by all the wonderful,
and very sensitive and soulful people who were the
singers, dancers, musicians, and actors in Harlem. . . ."

It was a time of awakening for black people in many

parts of the country and especially in Harlem. People were becoming restless. They were tired of the discrimination and lack of opportunity that seemed to be getting worse, even though sixty-five years had passed since slavery had been outlawed. There were race riots in several cities during the 1920s, and black leaders such as Marcus Garvey and W. E. B. Du Bois began exhorting the people to stand up for their rights and be proud of their heritage as black men and women.

Black people were also beginning to emerge in the arts, and many of them came to Harlem, which was the black cultural center of the country. Poets, writers, musicians, artists, singers, composers, dancers, and actors were looking for an opportunity to develop their talents and present themselves to appreciative audiences. For the first time, white people in America learned that there were serious black artists in many of the arts. Perhaps the most significant part of this cultural revolution was the emergence of jazz.

So Duke had company in his struggle. During his years in New York he met and shared ideas and aspirations with many other ambitious black artists. And just as in Washington, where he learned both from schooled and unschooled musicians, in Harlem he learned from both the intellectuals and the street people.

In 1931 Duke finally tired of the show-business routines of the Cotton Club and decided to strike out on his own. The Cotton Club and the entire Harlem period had been tremendously important to him. The years of stability had given him the time to develop his talents as a musician and a leader without worrying where the band's next date would come from. And the chance to grow with the jazz world in New York had put him into the mainstream of the new music.

When he arrived in New York he hadn't wanted to lead a band, preferring to play his piano, write some songs, and have fun. He became a leader almost by accident. Then the band grew, becoming three times as large as the original Washingtonians. With more musicians to work with and a need for more complex arrangements, Duke took an even stronger hand. Now the band was a big-time attraction and it needed a real leader. Duke took up the challenge. By 1931, the band was no longer the Washingtonians. It had become Duke Ellington and *His* Orchestra.

6

On the Road

Ellington's decision to leave the Cotton Club in 1931 was a risky one. The country's long era of prosperity had ended in late 1929, when prices on the stock market suddenly crashed. In the next two years, the economy got progressively worse, and by 1931 millions of people were out of work. Villages of tar-paper shacks grew up in parks and vacant lots, and people who had been prosperous a few years before were standing in line for free soup to keep from starving.

But somehow the entertainment world managed to survive. And Duke's decision to go on the road at least allowed him to go where the money was. He had the advantage that people all over the country knew his music. The band's recordings had been reaching large numbers of people. Their early radio broadcasts had also extended their audience. And during the years at the Cotton Club, manager Irving Mills had maneuvered some very important live appearances. The Ellington band had appeared on Broadway in a musical and a few prestigious vaudeville dates. They had even been to Hollywood to make a movie. All of these activities laid a solid groundwork for the band to strike out on its own.

So the Duke Ellington band became a traveling band,

crisscrossing the United States, and within a few years visiting even the most distant parts of the globe. Never again would it stay in one place for very long, and the road would become a way of life, night after night, week after week, year after year.

Travel was never easy. And it was particularly hard in the early 1930s. People who traveled long distances by train or bus had to get used to being uncomfortable. There was no air conditioning, and heating systems weren't always reliable. So it was hot in the summer and either too hot or too cold in the winter. Meals and sleeping accommodations were often poor and schedules often forced the band to travel all night and half the day between performances.

A black band found traveling difficult for other reasons, too. In the South, the segregation laws made it illegal for blacks to eat in white restaurants, stay in white hotels, even use white rest rooms. And accommodations for blacks were often miserable. In the North, discrimination was more subtle. There were no laws preventing blacks from moving about more freely, but in practice many places were actually off limits. The possibility of sudden humiliation always threatened a black band.

Duke knew there would be some anxious moments. So with Mills's cooperation he tried to avoid trouble in every way he could. At first he planned fairly short trips to cities on the East Coast where the band already had a reputation. Then the band traveled cross-country to California, returning to New York early in 1932 to appear at the prestigious Paramount Theater. It was the first black band ever to appear there, and the engagement was a great success.

For the second trip to California, Duke settled on a method of travel that would help the band avoid many pitfalls. He hired two private Pullman cars for the band to have all to themselves. When the Pullmans arrived in a city, they were shunted onto a siding and hooked up to water, sanitation, and electrical lines. There was a kitchen right on board, and there were berths for sleeping. The Pullman cars served as instant hotel rooms, providing a place to stay as well as a comfortable means of travel. Throughout his years on the road, Duke used private Pullmans for most of his long tours.

Early in 1932, Duke added trombonist Lawrence Brown to the band. Brown joined Tricky Sam Nanton and valve trombonist Juan Tizol, making a three-man section. Brown's impeccable tone and lyrical approach contrasted perfectly with Tricky Sam's growls. The Ellington band was the first to use three trombones and they gave Duke a wider range of possibilities than ever for his arrangements.

The band also employed a regular singer for the first time in 1932. Ivie Anderson became a traveling member of the group and added still another dimension with her sensitive interpretations of Duke's tunes. Other bands had begun to feature vocalists, and Duke felt some pressure to have one too. Ivie Anderson quickly proved Duke had done the right thing. Though he had a succession of female vocalists during ensuing years, critics and musicians generally agree that Ivie was the most sensitive and most talented of them all.

Then in 1933 the band got a chance to visit Europe. Duke was apprehensive at first because he didn't know how his music would be received there. Jazz had its roots in America—would Europeans like it or even care to hear it? The answer was yes. Of the band's first stop, England, Duke wrote, "We were absolutely amazed by how well informed people were in Britain about us and our records. They had magazines and reviews far ahead of what we had here, and everywhere we went we were confronted with facts we had forgotten, and questions we couldn't always answer. Nevertheless, the esteem our music was held in was very gratifying."

Even the Prince of Wales (who would soon become King Edward VIII) came to hear the band play. The Prince, an amateur drummer, was fascinated by Sonny Greer and all his equipment. Sonny remembered the evening well: "As soon as we had got the band set up, the Prince of Wales came over and sat down beside me Indian fashion. He said he knew how to play drums, so I said, 'Go ahead!' He played a simple Charleston beat, and stayed right by me and the drums through most of the evening. People kept coming up and calling him 'Your Highness,' but he wouldn't move. We both began to get high on whatever it was we were drinking. He was calling me 'Sonny' and I was calling him 'The Wale.' "

Duke's charm and grace impressed the English audiences, and all the concerts were sellouts. The critics, who were not used to American jazz, had both good and bad things to say about it. But the crowds were all wildly enthusiastic, applauding long and loud after most numbers.

In Scotland, then in Paris, the music was also extremely well received. Offstage, Duke was interviewed for magazines and newspapers. When questions were asked about racial conditions in America, Duke was careful with his answers, but he never avoided the issues. For instance, in Scotland he told a group of newsmen: "My contention about the music we play is that it is also folk music, the result of our transplantation to American soil, and the expression of a people's soul just as much as the wild skirling of bagpipes denotes a heroic [Scottish] race."

There were some minor disappointments on the tour. In England accommodations were all ready for Duke. But the rest of the band had trouble getting hotel rooms because some major hotels preferred not to accommodate black men. The band finally found rooms in a bohemian section of London similar to New York's Greenwich Village. Though there were few such incidents, they created some bitterness among the band members, who were forced to conclude that the prejudice of whites occurred all over the world.

Still, the huge popular success of the European tour gave Duke and the band great satisfaction. "That kind of thing gives you the courage to go on," Duke wrote. "If they think I'm *that* important, then maybe I have kinda said something, maybe our music does mean something."

When the band returned from Europe they resumed their travels back and forth across the United States. Sometimes there were Pullman cars to make things easy. Other times—on shorter tours—they traveled by bus or regularly scheduled train.

The band members soon discovered all of the drawbacks of life on the road. Any kind of tour was a rugged proposition, especially when it involved a series of one-nighters—a different town every day, different hotel,

The Cotton Club band, Duke Ellington conducting, 1931. Front row, left to right: Freddy Jenkins, Cootie Williams, Arthur Whetsol, trumpets; *Harry Carney, Johnny Hodges, Barney Bigard,* clarinets/saxophones. *Back row, left to right: Joe Nanton, Juan Tizol,* trombones; *Sonny Greer,* drums; *Freddy Guy,* banjo; *Wellman Braud,* bass.

The Ellington trumpet section, 1933. Featured at the microphone, left to right: Cootie Williams, Freddy Jenkins, Arthur Whetsol. Background: Duke Ellington, piano; *Sonny Greer,* drums; *Otto "Toby" Hardwick, Harry Carney, Johnny Hodges,* reeds; *Wellman Braud,* bass.

The Cotton Club Revue featuring singer Ethel Waters, backed up by Duke Ellington and his Orchestra.

Joe Nanton, Juan Tizol, Lawrence Brown.

The Ellington band on the road in Dallas, Texas. Irving Mills (*with hat on*) stands beside Duke. Johnny Hodges and Ivie Anderson stand in the doorway of the Pullman car.

different playing times. Travel schedules were often next to impossible. The booking agents treated the musicians like mechanical men. They figured the players would be there to perform no matter how far they might have to travel or how little time they would have to rest between stops.

Jazz pianist Billy Taylor recalls how physically demanding the road could be for musicians. "You get to your destination and find you don't have time to eat. You need a shave but you've got to change quickly. Everyone else is scrubbed and clean, and you feel you have the dirt of the road on you. It's really difficult. You sometimes don't have time to take care of personal cleanliness or eat or do any of the things one normally would do to get yourself to *feel* like performing."

This pattern, repeated night after night, week after week, was hard enough. But for those who were separated from loved ones, the travel was even harder.

"I have seen men on the bandstand so miserable it almost hurt me," Duke once said. "There are many occupations they would enjoy more, but, no, in music they can make a little more money. Being away from home at the wrong hour, or out of town where they can't watch over things, eats them up with anxieties."

Juan Tizol, long-time Ellington trombonist, had occasional bouts of "roaditis" as the years wore on. Finally, he couldn't take it any more. "I kept getting sick of the road and missing my wife," he said. "I could only be home once a year. So I had to leave. I used to beg Duke, 'Let me go home, let me go home. . . .' I used to ask him to let me go home for six weeks, when we were out this way [in California], and then I'd rejoin the band. This went on until I couldn't stand it any longer, and I said, 'I've got to leave you, that's all!' Oh, yes, I was getting older, but it wasn't that. It was the road. It was too long, and I couldn't take it."

A later Ellington musician, trumpeter Taft Jordan, remembered what a relief it was to leave the band: "When I left Duke, I was so tired I slept for almost a whole year. I had had too much road. For a long time I actually slept two or three times a day, and not cat naps, but for two or three hours. I hadn't realized how tired I was while I was out there."

Boredom was another hazard. Ray Nance, a trumpeter for the Ellington band in the 1940s, said the mental strain was harder than the physical. The waiting is what got to him—sitting around in a hotel in a strange town waiting to work four hours a night.

Of course there were diversions for men who were bored. A few had hobbies they could carry with them or friends to visit in one town or another. But one of the major diversions was drinking. Alcohol helped the men relax and contributed to many good times. But it also made life a living hell for some and ruined many promising careers.

Drinking had always been part of the music scene. Most early jazz players worked in a drinking atmosphere —in clubs, cabarets, and dance halls, where liquor flowed freely. A drinking audience was always conducive to drinking musicians. "No musician considered himself a jazzman if he didn't get drunk often and thoroughly," Sonny Greer recalled.

By his own account, Ellington himself was a prodigious drinker for many years. In sessions in Washington, a jug of corn liquor would be on the piano when the men started to play. The level in the jug would drop steadily, and when the jug was empty, another appeared to take its place.

"Liquor-drinking among the musicians was done from the gladiator perspective," Duke wrote, "in just the same way as when they challenged each other on their instruments. There were many who had big reputations, whose status was determined by the amount of liquor they drank, and accordingly, there were many contests."

Duke recalled one occasion when he refereed an all-night contest between Tricky Sam Nanton and trumpeter Rex Stewart, who was then with the Fletcher Henderson band. They ordered gin by the pint and drank it down without even grimacing. Duke matched them drink for drink. And in the morning he was still sober enough to guide them back to their rooms.

But around 1940 Duke gave up drinking almost altogether. "I don't drink any more," he wrote in his autobiography. "I retired undefeated champ about thirty years ago, and now I call myself a 'retired juicehead.' I drank more booze than anybody ever."

For some, drink became a curse. Trombonist Sandy Williams, who played briefly for the Ellington band in 1943, recalled his situation. "I loved it," he said of his time with Duke, "but during that time the bottle was really beginning to get to me. A drink will pick you up, but it gets to the point where you can't get on the bandstand unless you've got a bottle—in case you get tired. The road had a lot to do with it, because doing those one-nighters you were tired all the time, and back in those days the hotel accommodation wasn't like it is now.

You took a room wherever you could, even if it was in a barn. Some places, the hotels were so lousy I'd sleep in the bus. Traveling by bus, sleeping on it, just getting a sandwich here and a sandwich there, you were naturally tired all the time. Then you'd say, 'To hell with it! I'm going to get a drink.' "

The late Willie Smith, a big-band saxophonist of major talent, said, "I think drinking enters into it partly from boredom and lack of sleep. Up to a certain point, too, it speeds you up a bit, so far as your feelings are concerned. You feel more like playing. Then you find you need more and more whiskey to reach the same level. Over a certain point, it destroys your coordination, your thinking, and everything else. You finally end up a drunkard. . . . Drinking is an insidious process that finally traps you."

The problems of exhaustion, loneliness, boredom, and alcohol affected all traveling musicians. But black musicians had to live with one peculiar pressure—the constant threat of discrimination and racial hatred. The wings of Jim Crow followed them everywhere.

Almost every black musician who went South in those days had some harrowing stories to relate. Popular vibra-harpist Lionel Hampton recalled, "The black experience in music was a matter of heartaches, going hungry and even being beaten. Many a night, when we'd play in places like Waco, Texas, or Shreveport, Louisiana, we'd have to go to the bus station if we wanted anything to eat when we got through. And there they would close up the 'colored section.' Maybe, if we went behind to the kitchen, some old dishwasher with dirty hands might give us a sandwich. In the South, we couldn't go into a decent rest room. This was all part of jazz then. It got you emotional, and the next night it all came out in your playing."

Bassist Milt Hinton was another first-rate musician who experienced the horror of those days down South. He played in one Florida town where conditions would have frightened the bravest of men: "We would play a dance for white people, and they'd put a ring five feet back from the bandstand, so the people could stand but not get too close. There would be police in front of the stand, but the police didn't like us either. We were very sharp, dressed very neat, we were playing very good, and we all had money. After playing two hours, there'd be a half-hour intermission, and they'd put ropes through the hall for us to go outside. As we walked through this aisle, roped off on each side, with police in front and behind, these people would be swinging at us. We'd be ducking just to keep these guys from hitting us. They were showing off to their women."

This might sound exaggerated, but similar stories have been told by dozens of others. A successful band could pick its engagements more carefully, and, fortunately, conditions slowly changed. But it took a long time.

Another racial phenomenon, one that did not directly affect the Ellington band, was that of the mixed group, black and white. Roy Eldridge, a trumpeter of such considerable talent that he was nicknamed "Little Jazz," went on tour with the all-white Gene Krupa Orchestra. Eldridge told what happened, in an article for *Downbeat* magazine.

"We arrive in one town," Eldridge said, "and the rest of the band checks in. I can't get into their hotel, so I keep my bags and start riding around looking for another place where someone's supposed to have made a reservation for me. I have a heavy load of at least a dozen pieces of luggage. . . . When the clerk sees that I'm the Mr. Eldridge the reservation was made for, he suddenly discovers the last available room has been taken. I lug all that luggage back into the street and start looking around again.

"By the time that kind of thing has happened night after night, it begins to wear on my mind; I can't think right, I can't play right. . . . It was a lonely life. . . . It was as if I had leprosy. . . . One night the tension got so bad I flipped. I started trembling, ran off the stand, and threw up. . . . My nerves were shot.

"Man, when you're on stage you're great, but as soon as you come off, you're nothing. It's not worth the glory, not worth the money, not worth anything!"

Although life on the road seemed unendurable in many ways, the bands and the musicians continued to travel. There were good times and both personal and musical rewards.

The Ellington band always seemed to be among the most strait-laced and dignified. Their appearance, manners, and personal decorum were close to perfect. But there were times when even the Ellington musicians could cut up like a bunch of high school kids.

When Harry Carney joined the band in the late 1920s, he was only seventeen years old. The older players decided to have some fun. They were in Boston at the time and told young Carney there was going to be a party at the house of a woman named May. Since Carney was the new man, he was to buy the food and drink. Young Harry came to the address that the others had given him, burdened down with two full paper bags. As he entered the building, out came May followed quickly by a muscular man.

"So you're the guy who's been seeing my wife!" the man shouted.

When Carney saw that the man was carrying a gun, he dropped the bags and took off. The young saxophonist ran down the street, the burly man behind him, shooting the gun every few seconds. Three blocks away the breathless Carney ran into Bubber Miley, Tricky Sam Nanton, Otto Hardwick, and other band members. They were laughing so hard they could hardly stand up.

The whole thing had been a setup. The gun was loaded with blanks, and the local police had even been told in advance of the prank. It was an initiation Carney would never forget.

Other pranks followed down through the years. Freddy Jenkins liked to lick his mouthpiece when he was warming up. One night Otto Hardwick coated the mouthpiece with Limburger cheese and red pepper. Bassist Wellman Braud sometimes played the tuba, and one night some players filled it with water. Barney Bigard, who recalled the prank, was the victim of it. He sat just in front of Braud, so he was showered with water when Braud blew the horn.

This kind of prank could sometimes disrupt a performance, but Duke and other bandleaders realized that an occasional light moment kept the players relaxed, so they did not usually punish the pranksters.

Practical jokes aside, most of the musicians had serious reasons for putting up with constant travel. Being in a band like Ellington's, they had the chance to play their music almost every night and get paid for it. Ray Nance, the trumpeter who joined the band in 1940, put the travel in perspective: "If you're going to do what you want to do," he said, "you've usually got to sacrifice something. I like to play, and there's no type of music I'd rather play than Duke Ellington's. But playing involves travel, and, if you're married, every time you look around you're saying goodbye. Although it's part of the business, I don't like being away from my wife and home more than anyone else."

Other musicians were able to adopt a positive attitude toward the road, too. Saxophonist-clarinetist Russell Procope, who joined Ellington in 1946, explained that being a traveling man was part of the business. "The road is a way of life and you conform to it," Procope explained. "After a while, you get so you like it. Other people see you doing that and because you're not a nine-to-five guy they say you're crazy. They figure what they're doing is it. You know, you go to work at nine, get off at five, eat dinner, watch TV, and go to bed. I couldn't handle that. I couldn't handle that at all.

"People sometimes don't look at musicians in the right way. They lose sight of the fact that a musician is getting paid for what he does, just like everyone else. If you don't do it, you don't earn a living.

"The way I see it, things like traveling all over the world and meeting people in low places and high places, and all that, are fringe benefits. In fact, if more people had the opportunity to travel, to see what's going on around the country and around the world, other than their own small world, the whole world would be better off."

Although recording activity and record sales were hurt by the Great Depression, the Ellington band managed to do more recording than most groups. They averaged about nine recording sessions a year, keeping Duke busy as a composer and arranger.

In 1933 he wrote the hauntingly beautiful "Sophisticated Lady." The band's recording of it was a big hit, bringing in needed income and leading to additional recording sessions. A year later Duke wrote another hit—while waiting for a recording session to begin. He had three numbers ready but needed a fourth.

"The band ahead of us went into overtime," Duke wrote, "which gave me an opportunity to do my fourth number. So, standing up, leaning against the studio's glass enclosure, I wrote the score of 'Solitude' in twenty minutes. After we played and recorded it for the first time, I noted that everybody in the studio was moved emotionally. Even the engineer had a tear in his eye.

" 'What's the title?' somebody asked.

" 'Solitude,' answered Artie Whetsol, who had played so soulfully."

Both "Solitude" and "Sophisticated Lady," were striking ballads with memorable themes. And both were still bringing in royalties forty years later. In 1935, Duke wrote and recorded still another hit, "Sentimental Mood." His reputation as a bandleader had been growing and now he was being recognized as a first-rate songwriter as well.

The band finally headed South for the first time in 1934. Playing the theater circuit in Texas, they did four shows in one day, sometimes played for a dance after the shows, then picked up and moved to the next town. It was a rough grind, but the band traveled in their own Pullman cars, avoiding many of the problems they would otherwise have encountered.

"We made a lot of friends down there, and the climate and environment were conducive to the kind of musical dreaming I most enjoy," Duke said. After that, Southern tours became an important and annual part of the Ellington schedule.

Yet there were problems ahead. With the busy road schedule, Duke had taken even stronger control of the band, and some of the musicians resented it. The change was best described by Otto Hardwick, an original member of the Washingtonians. Hardwick had left the band in 1928 to form his own group, but returned to his old seat in 1932.

"When I rejoined the band," he said, "it was just like I never left. Except this way, maybe. It wasn't *our* thing any longer. It had become Ellington's alone. This was inevitable, I guess. Ten years ago it was '*We* do it this way,' and 'We wrote that.' Now, the we was *royal*. It seemed more inspiring, maybe more inspired, too, the other way, but I guess it all had to come to this. You love the guy right on. You have to admire him for all he's accomplished. You've got to be happy for him, he's that kind of guy."

Writer Barry Ulanov also described the resentments that developed in the band in the early 1930s. "Never had there been such a distinguished collection of jazzmen in one band," he wrote. And since they knew how good they were, there were "great shows of temperament, salary disputes, and lots of bewildering unpleasantness." The players had seen the band change from a collective organization to an organization directed by a strong leader.

In 1934 rumors began to circulate that seven men wanted to leave the Ellington band. These seven included the entire saxophone section—Johnny Hodges, Barney Bigard, and Harry Carney—bassist Wellman Braud, and three others. The musicians just weren't enjoying things as they had in prior years. They felt more like pawns than players. It was a major crisis. If the seven left, the band would be in a shambles.

Fortunately, there was no major rebellion. Bassist Braud eventually left, and Arthur Whetsol had to drop out because of illness. (Whetsol's place was taken by the very capable Rex Stewart.) But Ellington managed to hold the nucleus together. Although the players liked to complain about their situation, they finally decided to stay and the crisis passed. Still, the threat of half the band leaving at once must have caused Duke mountains of worry.

Duke had other worries, too. His mother became ill in 1933 and her health grew progressively worse throughout 1934, plunging Duke into a depression. By May 1935 Daisy was dying. Duke went to Detroit and sat at her bedside for the last three days of her life.

The Ellingtons had always been a very close family and the loss was very difficult for Duke to accept. "I have no ambition left," he confided to friends. "When mother was

alive, I had something to fight for. . . . Now what? I can
see nothing. The bottom's out of everything."

He was soon traveling with the band again, but no
longer was he looking forward to new places and new
people, and possible new triumphs. He was still mourn-
ing his mother. He tried to talk himself out of his
depression: "I would sit and gaze into space, pat my foot,
and say to myself, 'Now, Edward, you know she would
not want you to disintegrate, to collapse into the past,
into your loss, into lengthy negation or destruction. She
did not spend all the first part of your life preparing you
for this negative attitude.' " But it was some months
before he recovered. "I believed I could hear the
words, her words," he wrote, "and slowly—but never
completely—I really did straighten up."

Between his conversations with himself, Duke was
working on a new composition, a kind of memorial to his
mother. It was called *Reminiscing in Tempo.* It was
Duke's first extended work since *Creole Rhapsody,* and it
was recorded on four sides of the standard 78-rpm record.
Reminiscing in Tempo was never looked upon favorably
by most Ellington critics. But it seemed to sum up the
entire period from 1931 to 1935—a mixture of glad and
sad, triumph and tragedy. There had been a triumphant
tour to Europe, successful tours across the country and
the three hit recordings. But there had also been dissen-
sion in Duke's band, the illness of his friend Arthur
Whetsol, his mother's death.

The future of the band must have seemed uncertain,
too. The Depression continued and millions were still
unemployed. People who were working were earning less

than they had in the 1920s. Competition for the money people spent on entertainment was fierce, and musical fashions were shifting rapidly. In the summer of 1935, it seemed impossible to predict what future Ellington and the band would have.

7

The Swing Era

In August 1935, the band of clarinetist Benny Goodman played an engagement at the Palomar Ballroom in Los Angeles, one of the large dance palaces that were being built all over America. During the early nights of that engagement, the word began to get out to the teen-agers in Southern California that something new and exciting was happening at the Palomar. Soon there were crowds of people—both dancers and listeners—at every performance. Within months the craze for Goodman's band swept the country, creating a whole new, young listening audience for big-band music. The Swing Era had been born.

The word *swing* has several different meanings. One definition is that swing music gives the impression of getting faster and faster even when it really isn't. Another says that swing is music with a strong, pulsating beat that makes people want to get up and dance. In the mid-1930s, swing was associated with "big bands," the groups of fifteen or twenty that played for dances. A big band had trumpets, a reed section (clarinets and saxophones) of four or more, trombones, and a rhythm section (piano, bass, and drums). For the next five years, the big band was king. The full sound, the swinging solos, and the danceability of the music became the rage for the new generation of music fans.

Benny Goodman and his musicians were all white. And soon other white bands, including those of Artie Shaw and Tommy Dorsey, were in demand everywhere. These white bands got the big bookings and the major radio engagements. Their new fans often assumed that the bandleaders had invented the music they played.

The fact was, however, that the very idea of swing had come directly out of the black experience. And the development of big-band swing can be traced most directly to two black musicians: Fletcher Henderson and Duke Ellington.

Fletcher Henderson's original band had reached its peak in the late 1920s. It had twelve pieces: three trumpets, four reeds, two trombones, piano, bass, and drums. This instrumentation set the style for all the big bands that followed. Henderson had brilliant soloists, men such as Louis Armstrong, Coleman Hawkins, Jimmy Harrison, Tommy Ladnier, Joe Smith, and Buster Bailey. Henderson himself was a great arranger, and he also used arrangements by the brilliant Don Redman.

The Henderson band played at the Roseland Ballroom in New York until 1929. Nearly all the customers at Roseland were white and came there to dance. Henderson gave them music that was distinctly different from that of the white dance bands that also played there. He used fresh material, his arrangements were more inventive, and his soloists were spectacular. Most important, the band was swinging years before big-band swing was popular.

Henderson was playing jazz that people were able to

dance to. Unfortunately, he didn't have Duke Ellington's strength as a leader. After 1930, he had difficulty holding a first-rate band together, though he led various groups throughout the 1930s. In between bands he used his talents as an arranger and also sold some of the scores he had written for his own band. One of the leaders who made greatest use of Henderson's talents was Benny Goodman. So behind Goodman's sensational success in 1935 stood Fletcher Henderson.

The new young fans of swing flocked to hear their favorite bands in large dance halls and auditoriums around the country. Not everyone who came to the dance palaces wanted to dance; some gathered around the bandstand and listened. Some who came to the concert halls were not content to sit and listen. In 1938 the Goodman band became the first jazz band to play in Carnegie Hall in New York City. Young swing fans literally danced in the aisles of the famed concert hall.

The sudden attention given to white bands must have been discouraging to Duke Ellington and the other black bandleaders. Duke was considered a major musical figure by nearly all the white bandleaders, but at first his group couldn't cash in on his genius. The big problem was that the new swing bands were appealing to white listeners—those who had enough money to come and dance or listen. And in an era when there was still little contact between races, white fans were more comfortable coming to hear white groups.

Another problem was that most of the new audience had a limited knowledge of music. They jumped into the swing craze without knowing much about its musical background, and they naturally liked the white bands that had simplified and popularized swing music. The music that Duke's band was playing by 1935 was more subtle. His complex arrangements were harder to understand, especially for the young people just becoming aware of the music. And it seemed to those young fans that the Ellington band just *didn't swing!*

In truth, there were times when the Ellington band *didn't* swing. Duke loved ballads, and his longer compositions were often experimental. Other times, the band *did* swing, and the new young audiences began to find that out. Duke's bookings became more numerous, and fans learned to appreciate his special qualities. Slowly but surely, the Duke began catching on all over again. The band's tours continued, and there were also special events at which several of the big bands played on the same program.

Thanks largely to Irving Mills, Ellington's recording schedule was busier than ever. Mills had formed his own record company in 1936, so Duke did recordings with the full band and with smaller groups of sidemen. Thousands who couldn't see the band in person bought the records to listen and dance to.

Soon the big bands—black and white alike—were in great demand. They all traveled from coast to coast, often following each other into a particular town. On a Friday or Saturday night in the late 1930s hundreds of thousands were dancing to the live music of big bands in cities and towns from Maine to California.

The big-band musicians took great pride in their organizations. Promoters soon recognized that a battle between two or more bands would be a major attraction. Soon these "battles" to see which band could "cut" the others and come out on top were being scheduled in the larger dance pavilions. Supposedly the audience acted as judge, with its screams and applause. But the musicians themselves usually knew which band had won one of these competitions.

The Ellington band wasn't involved in many of these battles. Onstage competition wasn't really the Duke's style. This led some fans to believe that the band couldn't compete. But Duke proved when he did take part that his band could keep up with the best.

Chick Webb had a wild, swinging group that could cut almost anyone. And Webb's sidemen loved their reputation. Trombonist Sandy Williams, who played for Webb, remembered the time Duke brought his band into the Savoy Ballroom in Harlem for one of the famous battles.

"The battles at the Savoy were a big thing," said Williams, in *The World of Swing*. "[Webb] knew the crowd up there and everybody liked him, but we used to go into training like a prizefighter. We'd have special rehearsals. The brass used to go downstairs, the saxophones upstairs, and the rhythm would get together somewhere else. We had the reputation of running any band out that came to the Savoy.

"But just forget about Duke! The night he came, the place was packed and jammed, so you couldn't move. We opened, and just about broke up the house. After all, it was our crowd up there. Then Duke started, and he'd go from one tune right into another. The whole room was just swinging right along with him. I looked over and saw Chick sneaking around the other side into his office.

" 'I can't take it,' he said. 'This is the first time we've really been washed out.'

" 'You're right tonight, Boss Man,' I said. 'They're laying it on us.'

"They outswung us, they out-everythinged us."

There was also competition between individuals in a band. Harry Carney, Duke's great baritone saxophonist, felt that competition when he first joined Ellington in the 1920s: "When Duke first started writing for the baritone, I wanted to impress everyone with the idea that the baritone was necessary, and I very much wanted to remain a part of that sax section. There was so much competition . . . that I had to work hard. I liked the band and was always afraid of being fired. That was one school I enjoyed and didn't want to be expelled from."

Sometimes the rivalries were not so friendly. A classic case involved two talented tenor sax men, Herschel Evans and Lester Young, who played with Count Basie in the late 1930s. Evans played with a powerful, full tone, the way most tenor men of the day wanted to play. Young, on the other hand, had his own concept of tone, achieving a lighter, more breathy sound that Evans complained was all wrong. Both were outstanding soloists, yet their ideas differed greatly. Off the bandstand the two men associated with different groups of friends and rarely spoke to each other.

On the bandstand each said he couldn't bear to sit next to the other because of the difference in tone. Traditionally, the tenor sax players sat side by side. But Basie placed Evans and Young at opposite ends of the section, and used their rivalry to help build his blues-oriented arrangements. With the two tenor men constantly trying to outblow each other, the Basie band of the late 1930s became perhaps the swingingest group of all time. And even after Evans's untimely death in 1939, Basie continued to put two tenor soloists with contrasting styles at opposite ends of the section in order to carry on the rivalry and produce original and varied solos.

Once in a while, rivalries came out in the form of jealousy. Players who were featured on certain numbers treasured their solos and didn't want to give them up. Trumpeter Cat Anderson, who joined Duke in 1944, tells a story about his early days in the band. There was an arrangement of "Blue Skies" in which veteran trumpeter Rex Stewart ended the number with a rousing chorus. One night, when the band was playing in Ohio, Stewart didn't show up. Duke wanted someone to play the ending, but it was Rex's part and no one dared to volunteer.

"What about the new trumpet player?" Duke asked, looking directly at Anderson. Cat takes up the story from there.

"I told him I'd try, and after the other solos I came down front and played [Stewart's ending] an octave higher. When I ended up on a double C [a very difficult high note], and the people were applauding, Duke said, 'Good, we'll keep it just like that.' As luck would have it, Rex came in the stage door as I was blasting away. He didn't speak to me for fifteen years. He was high strung, and so am I."

As the Ellington band gained popularity at the end of the 1930s, most of the attention of the fans and the press was lavished on the soloists—Johnny Hodges, Cootie Williams, Tricky Sam Nanton, and others. Duke had encouraged such attention by writing special compositions or "concertos" for them. The best known were "Cootie's Concerto," also called "Echoes of Harlem";

"Barney's Concerto," also called "Clarinet Lament"; "Rex's Concerto," or "Trumpet in Spades"; and "Lawrence's Concerto," otherwise known as "Yearning for Love." These uncomplicated show pieces were an important part of the band's Swing Era repertoire.

But Duke finally felt that praise of his soloists had gone too far. He spoke out, revealing the resentment of his rhythm section—drummer Sonny Greer, bassist Wellman Braud, guitarist Freddy Guy—and the piano player. "Much has been said of the show part of the band—the melody instruments—" he said, "and I have grown a little tired of this perpetual eulogy, because everyone who really understands the dance band of today knows that it is the rhythm section which is by far the most important. Without a solid basis of impeccable rhythm, no matter how brilliant the melody section, the band can never be successful."

When bassist Braud left the band in early 1935, Duke replaced him with, not one, but two bass players, an almost unheard-of practice. It wasn't so much that one man couldn't fill Braud's shoes; it was just that Duke wanted an even stronger rhythmic punch coming from the section.

Then in 1939, Duke made a major addition to the band. One day a couple of his sidemen rushed into the Coronado Hotel in St. Louis and told him they had just heard a sensational young bass player at an after-hours gig. The three returned to the jam session, and Duke heard young Jimmy Blanton for the first time. As Duke said, "I flipped, like everyone else."

Blanton was not yet twenty years old. He had played only in local groups, some of them led by his mother, who was a pianist. At that time, Duke had one bassist. And the chance to get a musician of Blanton's talent couldn't be passed up.

"All we wanted," he said later, "was that sound, that beat, and those precision notes in the right places, so that we could float out on the great and adventurous sea of expectancy with his pulse and foundation behind us."

Duke made an immediate offer to Blanton, and he accepted. The addition of Blanton gave the band a pair of bassists again. But that didn't last long. Several weeks later, the other man just packed his bags and quit, telling Duke, "I'm not going to stand up here next to that young boy playing all that bass and be embarrassed."

Blanton took an instrument that had been limited to playing just four notes a measure (or as many notes as there were beats in the measure) and made it into a legitimate solo instrument, capable of the same kind of improvisation as any horn. He had the technique to play clusters of notes, in both his solos and rhythm accompaniment. Before long, every young bass player in jazz was trying to play like Jimmy Blanton.

"He had given us something new," said Duke, "a new beat, and new sounds. We made records of just bass and piano, and altogether it was a great period. Then he got sick, with tuberculosis."

Blanton's illness was a tragedy for the music world as well. He had been with Duke for less than two years when it struck. A short time later, in 1942, Jimmy Blanton died.

Blanton's sound can be heard on a number of the 1940–42 recordings on the Victor label, recordings generally considered among Duke's best. They include "Jack the Bear," "Ko-Ko," and "Morning Glory," as well as popular numbers such as "All Too Soon," "Warm Valley," and "In a Mellotone."

Although Blanton himself played with the Ellington band for a relatively short time, his style made a lasting impression, and Duke looked for other bass players in the same tradition. Very few musicians have made such a major contribution to music in so short a period of time.

Early in 1939, shortly before Duke discovered Jimmy Blanton, he made a discovery that was to have an even farther-reaching effect on the nature of his music. One night in Pittsburgh he was asked to listen to a young piano player and songwriter. Duke agreed in a half-hearted way, since he had many such requests every year. But as soon as he heard a song or two from the young man with the horned-rimmed glasses who sat at the keyboard, Duke jumped up.

"Man, you're great!" he said, immediately. "Play that again."

So the man played and sang some more of his original compositions as Duke listened intently. Finally he said, "Young man, I'm going to bring you to New York and you will be my lyric writer. I'm mad about what you're doing."

Duke had a show to do that night, and when it was over he couldn't find the youngster anywhere. But Duke learned that the young man's name was Billy Strayhorn, and he kept him in mind.

A short time later, in March of the same year, the young man showed up at the Adams Theater in Newark, New Jersey, where Duke was doing another one-nighter.

"You're not going to get away again," Duke told him,

and after the show he promptly took Strayhorn straight to his apartment in Manhattan.

"This is my home," Duke said, "and this is your home. I'm leaving for Europe in a few days, but you stay here. My son and sister will take care of you."

When Duke returned, the young man was still there. From that point on, they worked together until Strayhorn's premature death in 1967. Duke had originally been impressed with Strayhorn's words, but it was his talent as a composer and musical collaborator that made him so important. "Strays" turned out to be one of Duke's greatest blessings.

Musically, the two men were very close, their basic concepts and thoughts on the same wavelength. The younger man was always content to stay more or less in the background, but his influence was soon felt by everyone in the Ellington organization.

Billy Strayhorn hadn't even planned to be a professional musician. "Sure, I worked around, playing gigs," he said, "but I didn't consider myself good enough. I really didn't know what I was going to do. I even had some other jobs as a teenager. Music was just an avocation, not a vocation. The money I got for gigs was just play money to me. I thought no more about it. I just didn't consider making music my living."

But his hobby slowly became an all-consuming passion. So Strayhorn studied and worked, and studied some more. By the time he met Duke in 1939, he was well-trained as well as talented.

Like Duke, Strayhorn was a pianist, composer, and arranger. He served in all three capacities with the Ellington organization for nearly thirty years. The two men developed a deep friendship. As Otto Hardwick said: "Neither money nor business was an issue between them ever. Billy just wanted to be with Duke, that was all. It was love—a really beautiful thing."

There was really no formal working relationship between the two men. Strayhorn produced many of his own compositions and arrangements, most of which went into the band's book. He also collaborated with Duke on longer compositions. He sometimes traveled with the band, sometimes even relieved Duke at the piano for a few numbers. Other times he didn't go on tour but stayed behind to compose or arrange.

Some of the tunes most closely associated with the Ellington band were written and arranged by Strayhorn, including the band's new theme song, "Take the 'A' Train." Billy was also the composer of the beautiful "Lush Life," a ballad that many jazz musicians still love to play.

"Inspiration comes from the simplest kind of thing," Strayhorn told Stanley Dance in *The World of Duke Ellington,* "like watching a bird fly. That's only the beginning. Then the work begins. OH, goodness! Then you have to sit down and work, and it's hard. . . . You can't *tell* a musician a thought. You've got to elucidate, to put it on paper, *and* to communicate at the same time, which is *the* difficulty.

"The skill in arranging is how well you can put this down and have it come back. . . . It's the hardest thing in the world."

Billy explained that he and the Duke always took a great deal of time just to consider *how* to approach the piece. "The actual writing was nothing," he said. "You could do that overnight. It was the preparation that was tremendous."

For example, they once adapted part of "The Nutcracker Suite" by the Russian composer Tchaikovsky. "Arriving at the treatment we gave [the piece] was *agonizing,*" Strayhorn remembered. "It took six months. We went through it and played those pieces over and over again. We listened to them and talked about them. . . . But after we decided what to use and what not to use, and how to treat it—then you could sit down and do it in a day."

Duke always spoke and wrote about Billy Strayhorn with warm appreciation. "In music, as you develop a theme or musical idea," he wrote, "there are many points at which direction must be decided. And any time I was in the throes of debate with myself, harmonically or melodically, I would turn to Billy Strayhorn. We would talk, and then the whole world would come into focus. The steady hand of his good judgment pointed to the clear way that was most fitting for us. . . . Billy Strayhorn was my right arm, my left arm, all the eyes in back of my head, my brainwaves in his head, and his in mine."

Billy and Duke each had his own musical style. Stanley Dance observed: "Generally, you can tell the difference between Duke's things and Billy's. Duke's have a slightly more primitive (in the best sense of the word), more natural, less sophisticated quality. Billy's things are kind of polished. Duke's have a more spontaneous character. He always valued the more spontaneous element in jazz."

The arrival of Billy Strayhorn and Jimmy Blanton in 1939 brought the band near its peak as a creative musi-

cal group. Then early in 1940, one more new musician
completed the band. Tenor saxophonist Ben Webster had
made a guest appearance with the band five years earlier, and at that point Duke knew he wanted him. The
tenor sax was a popular solo instrument during the
Swing Era and Webster was one of the best, a big-toned,
imaginative soloist whose power was amply demon-
strated on both up-tempo tunes and ballads. When Duke
finally got him to join the band in 1940, Webster gave the
band its first major solo voice on tenor. His presence also
increased the sax section to five men, giving Duke still
another voice for his new arrangements.

Webster was featured on many of the top recordings
from the 1940–42 period. Duke himself cited the tenor
man's work on "Cottontail," "Conga Brava," "All Too
Soon," "Just a-Settin' and a-Rockin'," and "What Am I
Here For?" as prime examples of the Webster talents.

In November 1940, the band suffered a loss that
seemed sure to reduce its stature. The great trumpeter
Cootie Williams, who had replaced Bubber Miley eleven
years earlier, received a big offer to go with another band.
Duke reluctantly let him go, but how could he possibly
replace a Cootie Williams? However, Ellington's luck
kept him from having to think long about a replacement.
For on the very night after Williams's departure, Duke
heard Ray Nance play for the first time.

Nance was a fine trumpet man who could play both
open and muted horn. He could also play the violin, an
unusual instrument in a jazz band, and sing and dance,
making him valuable for special novelty numbers as
well.

So entering the 1940s, Duke's band was made up of the

veterans who had been there for years and the new-comers Blanton, Webster, Nance, whose immediate con-tributions were immense. Nance and Rex Stewart an-chored the trumpet section; Tricky Sam Nanton, Juan Tizol, and Lawrence Brown played trombone. The sax section had veterans Hardwick, Hodges, Carney, and Bigard and newcomer Webster. Blanton, on bass, was part of a rhythm section where Freddy Guy remained on guitar and Sonny Greer continued on drums. The piano player was Duke himself, with occasional relief from Billy Strayhorn. The band had stars at every position.

Duke continued to show his genius for making full use of the talents of individual musicians. Russell Procope, who joined the band in 1946, playing clarinet and saxo-phone for some twenty-five years, explained Duke's tal-ents: "Duke always had the reputation of having top personnel in his band. But that was because Duke used a man in a way best suited for that man's style. He *made* the personnel tops. For instance, in other bands, you went into the band and you played what was there, whether you fitted or not. It depended on you. If you weren't suitable for what was there, you had to leave.

"In Duke's band it was different. He fitted what was going on to you. It's like if you went to the tailor and got a suit. A 5–10 man couldn't wear a suit made for a man 6–10. It would look awful funny. So Duke would get a suit to fit the man."

Duke followed the same principle when writing for whole sections. Any arrangements for a section of trom-bones, trumpets, or saxophones would not be written for just *any* three trombones or five saxes. It would be written for the specific players in the band, taking advantage of their individual sound and abilities. While some bands played the same arrangements of their hit songs year in and year out, Duke was continually changing arrangements to take individual players into account. In fact, when a man left the band, the songs he had been featured in were put away, and Duke would eventually write something for the new man.

"A certain sound comes out of a big band," Duke said. "It may be in the character given it by a large brass section or by a particularly skillful group of saxophones. The minute you change the men in the section, it doesn't sound the same, although you may have the same arrangement."

Brooks Kerr, a young pianist who studies and plays Duke's music, pointed out that "other saxophone sections trying to play Duke's arrangements sound funny. You can switch bands with a Glenn Miller arrangement. But Duke's music was so personal and so individualized that you can't do it with his things. People have been trying for forty years, but something is always wrong."

For instance, as a general rule the baritone saxophone, the largest sax with the lowest range of notes, plays below all the other horns in the section. But because of Harry Carney's particular tone and ability, Duke would often have Carney playing a line above the tenors. With the Ellington personnel, it sounded fine. But if another band tried the arrangements with its players, this innovation just didn't work, because Duke's arrangement was written for Carney.

Duke's insistence on writing for individuals presents one basic problem today: without the original musicians, there can never be a live performance of Ellington works

The royalty of Swing—a king, a count, and a duke—1943. Benny Goodman, "the King of Swing," with Count Basie and Duke Ellington.

On the bandstand, 1943.

Duke Ellington and Billy Strayhorn at a recording session.

The reed section rehearses, early 1940s. Left to right: Barney Bigard, Ben Webster, Johnny Hodges, Otto Hardwick, Harry Carney.

The Ellington band poses for a publicity shot, c1945. Left to right behind Duke: Otto Hardwick, Juan Tizol, Shorty Baker, Ray Nance, Harry Carney, Kay Davis, Rex Stewart, Johnny Hodges, Chauncey Hooper, Ben Webster, Joe Nanton, Wallace Jones, Lawrence Brown, Sonny Greer.

that captures the genuine sound of the band. Duke's greatest legacy is not in music written down on paper, but in his records. By listening to the disks made through the 1930s and into the 1940s, a student can follow Duke's development and trace the changes in the band. By 1940, the sound had become deeper and fuller, sometimes making the band seem even bigger than it was. Duke also began to feature more interplay between sections and elaborate backgrounds for his soloists. When a player got up to solo, the rest of the band didn't stop.

Several of Duke's songs during this period used experimental forms. "Hip Chic," for example, is in the thirty-two-bar song form, yet has two sections of twelve-bar blues in it; "Buffet Plate" uses a twenty-four-bar chorus, while "Battle of Swing" uses a "concerto grosso" style, pitting a four-piece group against the rest of the band. Duke was trying new things while at the same time trying to please his audiences.

He also found time to record three numbers that became hits. "Azure" is a ballad, a mood piece featuring Barney Bigard on clarinet and Harry Carney on baritone. "Caravan" uses a Latin beat, and features solos by Bigard and Cootie Williams. "I Let a Song Go Out of My Heart" is a medium-tempo tune with a catchy, unforgettable melody line. Like "Caravan," it is still a standard today.

One other number bears mention here. It is "Diminuendo and Crescendo in Blue," a two-part composition that provided Duke with a chance to let his various sections work against each other. It was an experimental piece that Swing Era fans didn't really go for, though many critics thought it superb. But it's an important piece to remember, for it will return later to play a key role in Ellington's career.

In 1940 Duke and his long-time manager Irving Mills parted company. Duke continued to speak well of Mills, but he was ready to take a bigger role in scheduling and promoting the band. He had one of the greatest jazz organizations ever assembled, and in the next three years he gave live performances that old jazz fans still remember, and produced recordings that are considered masterpieces to this day. Duke had reached a sharp point of focus as a composer and arranger. He knew his personnel perfectly, since most of them had been with the band for years. The musicians knew what Duke was looking for, and they knew each other, which enabled them to function as a smooth-working unit.

The first of the landmark recordings came from a session in February of 1940. "Jack the Bear" was named for an obscure Harlem stride pianist and features Duke and Jimmy Blanton stating the theme, with subsequent solos by Bigard, Williams, Carney, and Nanton. "Ko-Ko" was described by one critic as "one of the monumental events in jazz music." Critic Albert McCarthy wrote, "The imaginativeness of the orchestration, the magnificent playing of the ensemble, with swiftly changing instrumental voices, and the striking plunger solo by Nanton combine to make it a masterpiece."

Later that year there was another showcase for Cootie Williams, just before he left the band. It was called "Concerto for Cootie," and later renamed "Do Nothin' Till You Hear From Me," an Ellington standard for years to come. Ben Webster was featured on a number called "Never No Lament," later retitled "Don't Get Around

Much Anymore," another Ellington standard. Duke was also writing and recording musical "portraits." Two of the best are "Bojangles," a portrait of Bill Robinson, a famous black dancer of the day, and "Portrait of Bert Williams," a characterization of the famous black vaudeville comedian. Finally there were the ballads and slow numbers, every bit as artistic as the up-tempo pieces. Two of the best from 1940 are "All Too Soon," which features Ben Webster, and "Warm Valley," featuring Johnny Hodges.

In 1941 Ray Nance carved a place for himself in jazz history with a brilliant solo on Billy Strayhorn's "Take the 'A' Train." Whenever that number has been played since, by the Ellington band or another, the trumpet solo incorporates some of Ray Nance's improvisations from the original recording. A 1941 session also produced the beautiful "I Got It Bad and That Ain't Good," with a touching vocal by Ivie Anderson and an equally sensitive saxophone solo by Johnny Hodges. More standards came out in early 1941, notably "Perdido" and " 'C' Jam Blues." All these recordings and many more produced by the Ellington band during that peak period are available today on long-playing disks. They are perhaps the most brilliant performances ever by a big band.

Neither Ellington nor the band could stay at that level of excellence forever. By mid-1942 world events and personal tragedies had taken the edge off their performances. Some critics believe that Duke's group never reached such a peak again. But the achievements of those few golden years mark one of the high points in the history of jazz.

8

Down Time

Duke Ellington and his band reached their greatest popularity during the so-called Swing Era, but they always stood somewhat apart from it, too. They could swing with the best bands of the day, and they appreciated the national excitement about big bands. But Duke was always an innovator. He wasn't content to do just what the others were doing. He continued to experiment with new sounds and arrangements. He featured ballads and novelty numbers as well as swinging up-tempo tunes, and not everyone approved. As critic Albert McCarthy wrote, "No matter what he contributed to the common pool of big band devices or what he had taken from it, from the beginning of his bandleading days, Ellington pursued a course that left him slightly outside the mainstream."

Duke's opinions about swing weren't all positive. In the late 1930s a reporter asked him about his place in the new music.

"Swing is stagnant and without a future, . . ." said Duke. "Most swing is like the monotonous rhythmic bouncing of a ball. After you hear just so much, you get sick of it because it hasn't enough harmony and there isn't enough to it."

"There is something lasting, however, to be obtained from the Negro idiom. I predict that Negro music will be alive years after swing is dead. Negro music has color, harmony, melody, rhythm. It's what I'm interested in, and I am going to stick to it. Let the others whirl and jerk . . . on swing, and let me sit back and drink in the music."

Duke was complaining about the huge amount of mediocre music that was being sold under the general heading of swing. There were so many bands around in the late 1930s and early 1940s that the crowds listened to, danced to, and applauded the good, the bad, and the mediocre alike. And although Duke was happy to be succeeding commercially, he wanted to avoid having the band labeled as just another swing outfit.

Fads and fashions in music change quickly. The Swing Era would not last forever. And the Ellington band itself couldn't last forever either in its current form. The so-called golden years for the band ended by the middle of 1942.

The band's problems were caused partly by changes in the music world. A long dispute between the record companies and the American Federation of Musicians caused the cancellation of all commercial recording from August 1942 until November 1944. No band, including Duke's, was able to make a single record for more than two years. The bitterness of the dispute and the loss of recording income caused serious problems for the band. Except for some radio transcriptions, there remains no record of any of the big bands during those years.

At the same time, the band was also deprived of its regular income from live performances. In December

1941, the Japanese had bombed Pearl Harbor in Hawaii, and the United States had entered World War II. During 1942 the whole country was mobilized for the war effort. Gasoline and many food items were rationed.

Trains and buses were crowded, and sometimes they didn't run at all, having been taken over to transport military men and supplies. Duke could no longer get his private Pullman cars. The band had to squeeze on crowded public trains or wait hours for a train to arrive. Life on the road, which was difficult in the best of times, now became nearly impossible.

Soon bookings began dropping off. People had less spare time, and less money. And since gasoline and tires were rationed, they couldn't go out as often. Bands had to take bookings whenever and wherever they could. It was a nerve-racking, wearing time.

The tragic illness and death of bassist Jimmy Blanton brought the first big change to the band. Then in mid-1942, exhausted by the hardships of wartime travel, veteran reedman Barney Bigard left the band. Bigard's sound and style could not be replaced. A year later Duke got Jimmy Hamilton, a fine musician in his own right, but very different from Bigard.

Soon after the recording ban ended, two other leading men left: saxophonist Ben Webster and trumpeter Rex Stewart. A year later, in 1946, Otto Hardwick, one of the original Washingtonians, gave up after nearly twenty-five years. That same year, trombonist Tricky Sam Nanton got sick while the band was on the road, and he died soon after. He was another who couldn't really be replaced. Some of the new men who replaced these old-timers would establish great reputations of their own: Jimmy Hamilton, Russell Procope, and Paul Gonsalves in the reed section and Cat Anderson on trumpet. But it would take years for them to develop. In the meantime, the band declined.

Before long, many other big bands were folding. Some lost out in the race for bookings. Others had been broken up by the war. And musical tastes were beginning to change. A group of younger musicians were beginning to experiment with new harmonies and different sounds. Some of these experimenters drifted in and out of the big bands, but they played mostly in smaller groups, developing a new style known as bebop, or modern jazz. Charlie Parker, Dizzy Gillespie, Kenny Clarke, Bud Powell, and others who first appeared in the early 1940s sent jazz in new directions.

In the midst of all these changes, Ellington managed to keep his band together and busy. When bookings were not sufficient to pay salaries, he would use his own income from royalties. But there were times when even that money was in doubt. The war year of 1943 had been particularly hard. One day Duke was headed for his agent's office to ask for an advance to meet his payroll. On his way he picked up his mail. He leafed through the envelopes until he came to one from RCA Victor, one of the companies he had been recording for. He tells the rest of the story in his autobiography.

"I opened it and took a quick glance at the check inside. The figure $2,250 is what I thought I saw as I slid it back in the envelope. To myself I said, 'Hey, if this is $2,250, I don't need to make this touch up here, but maybe my eyes deceived me and it's really $22.50.' So I pulled the check out again and it said $22,500! By the time I got my head back in my collar I was at the elevator exit on the first floor rushing to get a taxi. Man, what a surprise! What a feeling! I could breathe without inhaling or exhaling for the next three months!"

Neither the excitement of the Swing Era nor the difficulties of the war years kept Duke away from new ventures. In 1941, he had been invited to work on a theatrical revue called *Jump for Joy*. Years later he described the project with a touch of humor: "A team of scholarly Hollywood writers decided to attempt to correct the race situation in the U.S.A. through a form of theatrical propaganda. This culminated in . . . *Jump for Joy*, a show that would take Uncle Tom out of the theater, eliminate the stereotyped image that had been exploited by Hollywood and Broadway, and say things that would make the audience think."

With fifteen writers, the project became a nightmare. Numbers were being added and cut every day. And although the intentions of the writers were praiseworthy, Ellington felt that many things that needed to be said about the black experience were left out.

Jump For Joy opened on Broadway in the fall of 1941. It consisted of a series of sketches, songs, and production numbers. Duke wrote all the music and the entire band participated. Despite Duke's misgivings, the show was a big hit. But when the United States went to war, many of the young performers were drafted, and *Jump For Joy* closed after a run of three months. The show didn't bring Duke that many new fans, but the excitement of working in a new field always appealed to him.

In 1942, Ellington's new agent, William Morris, Jr.,

suggested he compose a long work for performance in concert at Carnegie Hall in New York. Benny Goodman had played there four years earlier, but none of the black swing bands had ever performed in the prestigious concert hall.

Duke agreed. The Carnegie Hall date would be an opportunity to contribute to the status of black music without the interference of a dozen writers. And it would be a chance to compose something new and innovative, without the restrictions imposed on the band in their dance-hall and club engagements.

In late 1942 Duke started to put things on paper. As usual, his working conditions were not ideal. He recalled in *Music Is My Mistress* that during a theater engagement in Hartford, Connecticut, he would get a few minutes between shows while the audience was watching the movie: "I would get my paper and pencil and go to the piano on stage and experiment and write. The light was not too good for writing music, and the movie they were showing was *The Cat Woman*. It was about a woman who used to change into a cat and do people in. Since I could see what was going on on the screen, it sometimes got pretty scary back there in the dark. But *Black, Brown and Beige* came off well nevertheless."

Black, Brown and Beige was the name of Duke's new work, and it was first performed at Carnegie Hall on January 23, 1943, before a standing-room-only crowd.

Black, Brown and Beige was Duke's most ambitious effort yet as a composer. He described it as a "tone parallel to the history of the American Negro." Each of the three sections told part of the story. *Black* dealt primarily with the past, and was built around work songs and spirituals. *Brown* depicted the various wars in which black Americans had participated, from the Revolution to the present. Duke said it was intended to recognize the "contribution made by the Negro to this country in blood." *Beige* portrayed the present day (as of 1943) and the black man's quest for solidarity and a more stable way of life.

Of course, the music served only as a symbol for the story. Duke made his statement not in words but in his choice and use of musical material from his heritage as a black man. Someone listening to *Black, Brown and Beige* without reading Duke's description of it might not see the historical parallels. But his devotion to his musical past would be clear in any case.

The piece ran almost an hour in its original version, and it provoked a great deal of controversy among the critics. The critics schooled in traditional music judged it by traditional standards. They were looking for the classic kind of form that evolved from white European music and they didn't find it. At the same time, jazz critics valued spontaneity and improvisation. They found too much form and not enough freedom.

So the critics' reaction to *Black, Brown and Beige* was mixed and confusing. One complained about the "symphonic bridges" between the "dance numbers" where Ellington gave up the strong swing beat. "If there is no regular beat there can be no syncopation, and thus no tension, no jazz," he said. Another writer praised the same passages, saying that they showed "how far Mr. Ellington has emancipated himself from the straitjacket of jazz formulas."

Some critics gave the Duke credit for "the sheer talent

that has gone into [the piece], the number, variety and quality of the ideas." But altogether they were confused. Ellington was writing music in a new form and there were no existing works to compare it to.

Duke originally recorded an excerpted version of *Black, Brown and Beige* in 1944, on four 78-rpm record sides. In the 1950s, he made a long-playing record of it, featuring gospel singer Mahalia Jackson. This haunting version of the work is still available today. And the main themes, "Work Song" and "Come Sunday," have been recorded many times by the Duke and others.

Despite the mixed reactions, the Carnegie Hall performance of *Black, Brown and Beige* served to separate Duke further from other jazz composers and arrangers. He was now considered in a class by himself. He was a bandleader whose group could swing with anyone and at the same time he was an innovative artist who was experimenting and searching for new forms of expression.

Black, Brown and Beige also reinforced Duke's commitment to the musical heritage of black people in America. From the days of Bubber Miley, he had encouraged his soloists to remember and express the black experience in their music. But during the Swing Era, the emphasis had been not on race but on the wide popularity of the swing band, especially among whites. Now, in 1943, Ellington reminded his fans and critics that his music was rooted in black America, not in the sudden craze for dance music. Years later, in the 1960s, when blacks had become angry, militant, and sometimes violent, Duke was accused of not having done enough for black people. Talking to writer Nat Hentoff during a 1965 interview, he replied, "People who think that of me haven't been listening to our music. For the past twenty-five years, social protest and pride in the history of the Negro have been the most significant themes in what we've done. . . . We've been talking about what it is to be a Negro in this country for a long time."

Duke continued to write concert pieces for the rest of his life. From 1943 to 1950, he presented a new, extended work each year at Carnegie Hall. The second concert, presented in December 1943, contained Duke's musical adaptation of Roi Ottley's best-selling book, *New World a-Comin'*, which looked forward to better conditions for blacks and all men after World War II ended. "I visualized this new world as a place in the distant future where there would be no war, no greed, no categorizations, no nonbelievers, where love was unconditional, and no pronoun was good enough for God," Duke wrote.

The critics continued to ask the same questions about Duke's music that they had asked earlier. Is this really jazz? Or is it classical music? Where does it fit in the overall musical scheme? Duke was impatient with such questions. He hated categories, and was not afraid to be a "one and only."

In December 1944, the Ellington band performed the four-part *Perfume Suite* at Carnegie, written by Duke and Billy Strayhorn. It was an impressionistic mood piece, hardly appealing to swing fans. Even some of the players didn't like it, since improvisation was at a minimum.

In 1946, Duke premiered the *Deep South Suite*, another four-part mood piece. The last section, "Happy Go-Lucky Local," portrayed a train in the South, "not one of those luxurious, streamlined trains . . . but a little train . . . that was never fast, never on schedule, and never made stops at any place you ever heard about."

Like many of Duke's longer compositions, *Deep South Suite* went unrecorded. Only "Happy Go-Lucky Local," an outstanding, rocking, swinging piece, was ever recorded by the band. Ironically, its melody was picked up almost note-for-note later and made into a big rock-'n'-roll hit, "Night Train."

The 1947 Carnegie Hall concert was another landmark in Ellington's career. He had been commissioned by the government of Liberia to compose a piece of music to commemorate the African country's centennial as a republic. *Liberian Suite* consisted of an introduction, "I Like the Sunrise," sung by Al Hibbler, and five contrasting dances that used African rhythms and primitive sounds. It was later recorded and is available on record today.

By 1950, Duke wrote, "everybody was giving concerts, and even a concert at Carnegie Hall no longer had the prestige value it had had in 1943, but our series there had helped establish a music that was new in both its extended forms and its social significance."

The Carnegie series also served once and for all to set Duke apart from his contemporaries in jazz and swing. Most critics agreed, whether they liked his music or not, that he was more technically and musically advanced than anyone in his field. On one hand he was compared to Count Basie, Fletcher Henderson, and other big-band leaders. But he was also beginning to be compared with the major "legitimate" songwriters of the day.

The 1920s and '30s had been a golden age for musical theater in America. Shows written by Harold Arlen, Cole Porter, Jerome Kern, and others provided dozens of songs that have become "classics," or standards, even today. Ellington, too, wrote songs that belong in that class.

Perhaps the most interesting comparison to Ellington in the field of songwriting is George Gershwin. Gershwin was born in 1898, a year before Duke. Both became top songwriters, and both wrote long experimental pieces. Gershwin, deeply influenced by black music and jazz rhythms and harmonies, wrote the famous *Rhapsody in Blue, An American in Paris,* and the opera *Porgy and Bess,* which was about black people and was produced with an all-black cast. *Rhapsody in Blue* was written in 1923, when Gershwin was just twenty-five years old. He died in 1937, just as Duke was beginning to gain national recognition.

Ellington matured as a composer more slowly than Gershwin. One reason was that Gershwin had opportunities that Ellington lacked. Duke never got the opportunity to do a big Broadway musical, for example. As jazz pianist Billy Taylor commented, "Gershwin, as a white artist, had avenues open to him that Ellington, as a black artist, did not. The blacks just didn't become established [on Broadway] in the 1920s as the Gershwins, Cole Porters, guys like that did. And because Duke didn't have these avenues open to him, his development was slower."

Duke did have some great advantages, though. Taylor pointed out that Gershwin "was a frustrated jazz player" and that he and other Broadway composers "would come up to Harlem for sessions" with Fats Waller, Ellington, and others. Duke learned the new music at first hand. Gershwin learned and used it at second hand.

When World War II ended in 1945, economic conditions began to improve quickly. But there was no real resurgence of big-band activity. Big bands continued to fold, and small bebop groups began to attract young jazz fans to new, small night clubs. There were no more big dances, big theater engagements, no more youngsters gathering by the thousands to scream and yell. Tastes were changing. The Swing Era was over.

In 1946 and '47 the bands of Benny Goodman, Tommy Dorsey, Benny Carter, and Woody Herman all folded. Morale in the Ellington band was low, and Duke anxiously awaited his royalty checks so he could pay the men. But he still didn't think of quitting.

Then in 1948 there was another dispute between the American Federation of Musicians and the record companies. For a full year no new recordings could be made. To make matters worse, early in the year Duke began feeling ill. He learned that he had a cyst on one of his kidneys that had to be removed by surgery. When he left the hospital, he went to England to recuperate, taking only trumpeter Ray Nance and a singer, Kay Davis, with him. He kept the band on payroll, but gave them some time off.

In England he rested, then made a few appearances with Nance and Davis. But rumors began filtering back from the States. His band members were playing on their own and succeeding. Ellington began to worry. It seemed that when he returned to America there might not be an Ellington band.

9

"Newport Up"

The rumors that reached Duke in England had some basis in truth. Some of the band members had been working on their own. Johnny Hodges recalled the details, in *The World of Duke Ellington.*

"Well, while we were laying off, Russell Procope and I came to Atlantic City with our wives for a little vacation. One night, we decided to go to the Belmont to hear Wild Bill [Davis]. He invited us to a jam session, so we took our horns and we jammed and jammed, until seven or eight in the morning. . . . A couple of clubowners from New York heard us. One of them had the Apollo Bar on 125th Street, and when we got back he approached me about getting a little band together. So Billy Strayhorn, Tyree Glenn, Jimmy Hamilton, Sonny Greer, Al Hibbler, and I went in there, and we got very lucky, and started putting 125th Street on the map again. Later on, we added Junior Raglin on bass, and we stayed there for seven weeks, until Duke came back."

The Ellington sidemen were all well known by then and could obviously make it on their own. They could play the things they liked in a smaller group without the confinement of Duke's scores and arrangements. They were swinging all the time and enjoying it.

But all the years with Duke also meant something to

these men. When Duke got home, he went to the Apollo Bar. He wanted to know if his top men were breaking away. Hodges recalled the ending of the incident: "We were loyal, and we broke our band up, and came back."

The band was back together, but the future was not promising. By 1948, big bands were nowhere. The crowds and enthusiasm of the Swing Era had disappeared. There was still a group of jazz fans, but they gravitated toward the smaller, modern bebop bands. Ironically, another group of fans had rediscovered New Orleans–Dixieland jazz. Many of the old New Orleans performers, who had been unable to earn a living in music since the late 1920s, were playing once again.

This left Duke in the middle. He had already had a long and successful career and a secure reputation as a songwriter and composer. But he had no audience; his sound was too old for the bebop fans and too new for the Dixieland crowd. He could have broken up the band and concentrated on his composing. But Duke refused even to consider this possibility. After all, how could he hear his compositions if he didn't have his band?

"It's a matter of whether you want to play music or make money," he once said. "I like to keep a band so I can write and hear the music the next day. The only way you can do that is to pay the band and keep it on tap fifty-two weeks a year. If you want to make a real profit, you go out for four months, lay off for four, and come back for another four. Of course, you can't hold a band together that way and I like the cats we've got. So, by various little twists and turns, we manage to stay in business and make a musical profit. And a musical profit can put you way ahead of a financial loss."

A musical profit! In a way, that was the central theme of Duke Ellington's career. It was the music, above everything else, that concerned him. He didn't break up the band and he didn't even cut its size.

So the band went back on the road, hustling for bookings and surviving on royalty income when necessary. But they were sluggish and depressed much of the time. The men knew they had fallen upon hard times, and the departure and arrival of players kept Duke from putting a top band together again. When they returned to the recording studio in 1949, the results were uninspiring. Another problem was that recording executives worried about Duke's declining popularity and insisted that he record the old standards. If a band wasn't packing them in, it was harder to experiment.

Duke hated to see an established player leave him. In fact, he really couldn't face it, and preferred to believe the man was taking a leave of absence. "He'll be back," Duke would say whenever one of his favorites departed.

Duke's faith was tested severely in 1951. The band was still having a tough time when Duke got the word that saxophonist Johnny Hodges, trombonist Lawrence Brown, and the inimitable Sonny Greer would be leaving to form a small group. This time it was for real. Hodges and Brown, of course, were two of Duke's headliners. Greer, besides being a fine drummer, was the last of the original Washingtonians. (Freddy Guy, the guitarist, had left in 1949 and was not replaced.) Now, only the leader carried on.

Fortunately, Duke's "he'll-be-back" philosophy proved to be mostly right. Hodges did return, in 1955, and stayed until his death in 1970. Brown came back in 1960, and remained for another decade. Greer, however, had had enough and confined his activities to small groups in and around New York.

Duke's immediate problem in 1951 was replacing his departed friends. He hired the talented Willie Smith to play in place of Hodges. To replace Greer, Duke hired Louis Bellson, the first white musician ever to sit in the band. Bellson was not only a fine musician but also had a powerful personality, and he got along well during his stint with Duke. After that, Duke hired white sidemen from time to time, and there was trouble just once. In 1953 white clarinetist Tony Scott joined the band, then quit after a month, claiming the attitude of one or two band members made it impossible for him to stay. And Duke himself admitted that Scott was "the only musician who was ever forced out of my band by race prejudice."

By the mid-1950s, the Ellington band was carrying on almost alone. Even Count Basie had temporarily broken up his big band (he organized another a year or two later). Duke was playing wherever he could get an engagement and he had to bend over backwards to please his audience. The band did more standards than usual, big-band arrangements of current hit tunes, and novelty numbers. It was the kind of program they'd never have done in the past. Even the royalty income was dropping. Duke's last song hit, "I'm Beginning to See the Light," had been written in 1944. He searched desperately for ways to renew the band's popularity without much success.

The power of the band was still there. Willie Smith, the new man in the sax section, recalled one occasion during an engagement at New York City's Birdland in the early 1950s when the old excitement and sense of style returned. "Some spark got into them and for six months the band was unbelievable," he said. "It had so much fire and determination—every set, no lulls, no letdowns. People used to get up in the middle of a number at Birdland and start yelling. They couldn't contain themselves and wait until the end of the number to applaud."

But more often, the band played lackadaisically, the performers drinking between sets and generally goofing off. One major problem was the audiences. They came now and listened respectfully, but the old enthusiasm was gone. The Ellington band seemed a part of history, no longer an important part of the musical mainstream.

Jazz itself was taking another new direction. Bop had been followed by "cool jazz," which was characterized by a light, airy tone and a relaxed style of play—the complete opposite of the wailing intensity of bop. The newest jazz was sophisticated and appealed especially to college students. It was performed in small cabarets and coffeehouses, and was sometimes used to accompany readings of poetry. Colleges were inviting more and more jazz musicians both because jazz was popular and because it was by now a respected art form. But the new small groups got most of the bookings.

While jazz was prospering among its small group of fans, another musical craze was being born. Like jazz, it grew from black music, and like swing, it was first made popular by a white performer. The music was called rock-'n'-roll, and its first great star was Elvis Presley. Compared to jazz or even to the swing bands of the 1930s, early rock-'n'-roll was very crude and simple both in rhythm and harmony. It was elemental and shocking to some in much the same way Bubber Miley's "jungle music" had shocked listeners in 1920s. But the rock-'n'-roll fad promised no help to Duke and the band.

On the bright side, jazz was being taken more seriously in the 1950s. For the first time it was being studied and analyzed by serious students of music. Many of the young jazz players had studied at the conservatory level, much the same as a young classical musician would. So in that sense, jazz was achieving new levels of sophistication. Changes in the recording industry also brought a wide range of jazz to a large new audience. The long-playing 33 1/3-rpm record enabled companies to put as many as fifteen old 78 recordings on a single disk. They put out anthologies that would introduce new listeners to jazz and its history. And they reissued albums of vintage recordings made by individual artists, including the Ellington band.

Duke continued work on experimental pieces whenever he had the opportunity. In 1951, for instance, he had done a fine recorded version of *A Tone Parallel to Harlem,* an extended work still considered among his best. And in 1955 he was commissioned to write a piece to be played by the Symphony of the Air, a classical orchestra, in concert with his band. The result was a long piece called *Night Creature,* a mood composition in which each of three movements described a different creature—a fantastic insect, a monster, and a woman. Though there was no widespread public audience for *Night Creature,* the band played it with symphony orchestras in Buffalo, Detroit, New Haven, and Washington, D.C.

By 1956, the personnel in the band stabilized for a time. Johnny Hodges had returned after four years away, and the sax section was again an outstanding unit. Tenor man Paul Gonsalves (a disciple of Ben Webster) was receiving increasing attention. Jimmy Hamilton, originally hired to replace Bigard, had been with the band for thirteen years. Russell Procope had ten years' experience, and old-timer Harry Carney was still holding down the baritone spot. Ray Nance was the veteran of the trumpet section, and he was joined by high-note specialist Cat Anderson, Willie Cook, and a dynamic modern player named Clark Terry. Quentin Jackson and Britt Woodman did a fine job on trombones. Sam Woodyard was the new man on drums and a good one, and Jimmy Woode was the current bassist. The piano player remained the same.

The band was playing well, better than it had played a few years earlier, but it had not found a way to restore its old popularity. Count Basie had reorganized his band, and his free-swinging style began to catch on. Some were predicting a revival of interest in the big bands, but nobody could know for sure.

One of the important new developments in jazz in the 1950s was the jazz festival. Usually held outdoors for a few days or a week in the summer, a festival brought together most of the top jazz people in the country, from Dixielanders to modernists. Real jazz fans could come and see almost everyone in the same few days. The first of the festivals, organized by George Wein, took place at Newport, Rhode Island, a historic summer resort.

The Ellington band was invited to the Newport Festival for 1956. Duke's men would appear on a program with other groups that were more important in drawing a crowd. Still, Newport was an important engagement. As part of a sort of live anthology of jazz, the Duke would be a spokesman for the big band. And a good performance there, with the recording engineers catching every note, might improve the band's bookings and make life a little easier.

Duke understood the importance of the event and prepared carefully for it. As had become his custom, he wrote a special composition, *The Newport Jazz Festival Suite*. A medium-tempo opening section, "Festival Junction," was followed by a slow, blues-oriented middle section, "Blues to Be There," and an up-tempo finale, "Newport Up." It was designed to show off the entire band in ensemble and section work, as well as many of Duke's fine soloists. He was hoping the *Suite* would help put the band back in the public eye. He also planned to do "Jeep's Blues," which featured a long solo by Johnny Hodges, and an old-timer from 1937 called "Diminuendo and Crescendo in Blue." Duke had performed this vintage piece at Birdland in New York some months before. At that time tenor sax man Paul Gonsalves had asked Duke if he could take a few choruses of improvisation between the first and second parts. Duke agreed, and when they played the number, Gonsalves got up and played chorus upon chorus. The Birdland crowd had loved it. So Duke decided to try it again at Newport.

Duke's was the last band to go on that night. The crowd of 7,000 had already had several highspots that evening and they were beginning to get a bit restless. *The Newport Festival Suite* and Hodges's long solo in "Jeep's

Blues" were well received. The listeners seemed respectful and appreciative, but they were not wildly enthusiastic. If the Duke was going to make any major impression, he would have to do it with "Diminuendo and Crescendo in Blue."

At the outset the band started cooking. They swung their way through the opening section and seemed to have the full attention of the crowd. Then Gonsalves stepped out in front of his stand, raised the mouthpiece to his lips and began to blow.

Duke had told his tenor man, "Take as many choruses as you like." But Gonsalves knew it was important to know when to stop. "The length is really determined by the way the rhythm section is working and everything is building up," he said later. "The climax may come after ten or after five choruses, but if you go beyond it you destroy everything."

This night, Gonsalves was in top form. He was on top of the beat, varying his techniques, not honking or squawking or trying to showboat. Duke, drummer Sam Woodyard, and bassist Jimmy Woode made the beat even stronger. The whole band seemed to pulse with the feeling. They were swinging.

One chorus led to another, then to another, then another. And with each one, Gonsalves built up the excitement, the urgency in his playing. After the tenth chorus or so, the audience realized something was happening, something unplanned and completely spontaneous. They began swinging with the band. Some people started dancing in the aisles, others clapped their hands to the beat, still others just shouted encouragement to

Gonsalves, who was digging in and blowing harder and harder. The entire crowd of some 7,000 jazz fans was suddenly one, all riding with the Ellington band.

Gonsalves played for twenty-seven choruses, a miraculous feat. And when he finished, Duke and the band jumped in with no hesitation. Duke himself took a brief, swinging solo, then the entire band rocked the number to a shouting conclusion, with trumpeter Cat Anderson blowing high, screaming trumpet notes above the entire band. The crowd was on its feet, cheering and stomping. It was a happening in the true tradition of jazz, a spontaneous performance that carried the crowd to ecstasy. Even today the recording of the event can make a listener stomp and shout.

The next day the whole jazz world was talking about the Ellington band and Gonsalves's amazing performance. It was just the tonic Duke needed. Soon afterward his picture appeared on the cover of *Time* magazine, and the album of the Newport performance became his first best-selling, long-playing record. Requests for band appearances began rolling in. Clubs, colleges, and concert halls all asked for Duke Ellington. New recording dates were hastily arranged. Ellington was back in the spotlight, all because of one thundering, swinging performance. Never again would he have such tough, uncertain times as the early '50s.

Suddenly people outside of the business began realizing what contributions Duke had made to music. His old recordings were reissued on new, long-playing records. Younger critics and students of music began tracing his development. They rediscovered the excellence of the band during the golden years of the early 1940s and

realized how many of the standard tunes belonged to
Ellington, Strayhorn, and the band. And they began to
reexamine his longer works and appreciate his genius as
an arranger.

Duke was about to enter not only the busiest but also
one of the most productive periods of his life—a time
when he'd finally begin to receive the recognition he so
richly deserved.

This latest success came when he was approaching his
fifty-eighth birthday. The majority of men at that age are
thinking about retirement, perhaps some years of leisure,
if they're lucky, to do some of the things they've never
had time to do before. Not Duke Ellington. He never gave
a single thought to retirement. He welcomed his latest
success and the possibilities it brought to him. Whenever
anyone mentioned retirement, Duke would look the person straight in the eye and reply: "Retire to what?"

10

World Traveler

People who worked or traveled with Duke Ellington were continually amazed at his energy. After Newport the band was booked solid, traveling not only in the United States, but spending more and more time overseas, where enthusiasm for jazz was reaching new highs. Duke was approaching sixty, but he never slowed down.

"Musicians less than half his age have marveled at his ability to drive or fly hundreds of miles a day to a gig," wrote Leonard Feather, "sit up after the job talking with friends, or composing, go to bed at 9 A.M., rise at 4 P.M., eat a steak breakfast, and be cheerfully prepared to meet his public at 8:30 P.M., then leave at 2 A.M. for a one-man stand in another state or another country."

Stanley Dance also made note of Duke's grueling pace. "As far as I'm concerned," Dance said, "there's no real explanation as to what drove him. He had a lazy streak, too. But this drive is something you're born with. A lot of the times it was a matter of working and keeping the band working. That band meant a lot to him, to have that instrument. You've got to do all sorts of things to keep a band like that working. It's no accident that it survived as it did.

"And Duke's schedule was always tougher than any-

136

one else's. When I was in South America with the band in 1971, for instance, everyone was exhausted. He was the oldest one on the tour and where everyone else would get off the plane and flop in a hotel to get a couple of hours sleep, he'd be doing press interviews, or radio shows, or TV shows. He had far more to do than anybody, and he did it."

The older members in the band could recall several earlier trips to Europe. In 1933 they had created a sensation in England, Scotland, and France. Then in 1939 they went again, but this time Europeans were tense and unhappy because war with Nazi Germany seemed near. The tour began in France. Then, after performances in the Netherlands, the band was to go to Denmark by train through northern Germany.

The German government under Adolf Hitler was racist, claiming that blacks and Jews were inferior to white "Aryan" peoples. And it did not like jazz. The band was nervous and determined to keep a low profile during the ride.

Once they were settled on the train, a couple of German youths noticed Cootie Williams's record player and asked him if he had any jazz records. He gave them some and they listened all afternoon. The language of jazz knew no boundaries even then.

In 1948, when Duke was recovering from surgery, he made his second visit to England, with Ray Nance and Kay Davis. And the whole band had gone to Europe again in 1950. On that trip Duke decided to play some of his new compositions in Paris for the usually hip French audience. He and the band went into *The Liberian Suite,* which the French had never heard. Between movements of the *Suite*, a young man walked down one of the aisles and approached Duke.

"Mr. Ellington," he said, politely. "We came here to hear Ellington. This is not Ellington!"

So Duke changed the program and for the rest of the evening the band played standards from the 1930s and early '40s. This kind of reaction happened more and more often during the 1950s, and it put Duke in a difficult situation. On one hand he wanted to please his audiences. But on the other hand he did not want to let the band become a museum piece, playing only music from an earlier day.

After the great success at Newport, the band's international travel really began. They went to Leeds, England, for a special festival appearance in 1958. In 1959 Duke was asked for the first time to do a movie score. The film was *Anatomy of a Murder,* directed by Otto Preminger and starring James Stewart. Duke was featured in a small role as a piano player. That job led in 1960 to another movie score, for a picture called *Paris Blues,* starring Paul Newman and Sidney Poitier. Duke traveled to Paris, where the movie was being filmed.

The band toured Europe again in 1962 and in 1963. In the fall of '63, the United States Government asked Duke and the band to make a special tour of Asia and the Middle East. Duke readily accepted. Some of his fans wondered why he hadn't been asked earlier.

In 1958 the State Department had decided to send a jazz band to Russia for the first time. Instead of sending Duke or Count Basie, it sent Benny Goodman, who had to put together a special band for the occasion. Many believed that Ellington and other black musicians had been passed over *because* they were black.

Duke was past the point of worrying about these things. If the government wanted to send Benny Goodman, it was fine with him. But when they called in 1963, he went without hesitation. The tour began in Damascus, Syria. Duke was a keen observer wherever he went, and clearly enjoyed encountering new people and places, sights and sounds.

A tour sponsored by the U.S. State Department differed from the band's private tours. Now the musicians were representing their country and they had to learn to become diplomats. On arrival in Damascus, for instance, they were assembled in the garden at the U.S. embassy and briefed on the country, its customs, and its standards of behavior. They learned, for example, that in Syria it was an insult if you showed the sole of your shoe while talking with someone.

The band played three or four concerts a week, and every member was expected to attend receptions and other official gatherings. They were encouraged to speak freely about the United States. "As citizens of a free country," Duke noted, "there are no restrictions on our tongues. We are to speak as free men."

Duke always spoke his mind and couldn't be told what to say. There was a press conference in every city the band visited and the questions sometimes took a rather difficult turn. "At the press conferences," Duke recalled, "we would talk about jazz, and very often, the race situation in America. Some of [the reporters] wanted information, but others wanted to discuss [the problem] from a more provocative viewpoint. . . . I always told them that the Negro has a tremendous investment in *our* country. We have helped to build it and we have invested blood in every war the country has fought. . . .

"One man asked me, 'Why hasn't the Negro artist done more for the cause?' That upset me and I said, 'If you knew what you were talking about, you wouldn't ask a question like that.' I came back to him later, after I had cooled off a bit, and explained that we had been working on the Negro situation and his condition in the South since the 1930s, that we had done shows, musical works, benefits, etc., and that American Negro artists had been among the first to make major contributions."

Duke learned to handle the press conferences very well. But the main business was the music. People everywhere were anxious to hear the band and to meet and talk with the musicians about their art.

In addition to regular performances, Duke arranged "lecture demonstrations." Duke and a few of the sidemen would appear and play informally, and Duke would talk between selections about the music—its roots, its history, its ideas.

From Damascus the band traveled to Amman, Jordan, where they played in an amphitheater that had been built into the side of a hill several thousands years ago by the Romans. They continued to Jerusalem, then to Kabul, Afghanistan. During the concert there, Duke noticed a military hero, known as the Victor of Kabul, in the front row. "As I do my finger-snapping bit at the end of the concert," Duke reported, "I find that the Victor of Kabul's finger-popping pulse and mine are together. We are swinging!"

In India, Duke and his men listened to Indian music and instruments, and in Ceylon they saw a demonstration of native dances and drum rhythms. Then they were off to Pakistan, Iran, Kuwait, and Baghdad, Iraq. There the band was almost caught in political violence. The home of a government official, not far from the hotel where the band was staying, was bombed during the night.

The tour was in its eleventh week when it ended suddenly and unexpectedly in Ankara, Turkey. Duke was about to have dinner when he received a phone call. A State Department officer said there was an urgent message. He came up to the Duke's room and announced that President John F. Kennedy had just been assassinated.

"The food just sits there and gets cold," Duke wrote. "Nobody eats, nobody talks, nobody does anything for thirty minutes. When the news hits the city, it apparently has the same effect on the crowds in the street. The people all look as though they are numbed.

" 'Well, that's the end of the tour,' I finally say, for we are in a land where they normally mourn forty days." Scheduled appearances in Cyprus, Egypt, and Greece were canceled and the band flew home.

The Asian tour confirmed that jazz was achieving a world-wide reputation as an American art form. Only forty years earlier it had been considered vulgar and frivolous. The trip also opened the gates to more trips. In the next ten years Duke and the band traveled to Japan, Latin America, Russia, Eastern Europe, and Africa.

A high point of these travels was Duke's visit to Dakar, Senegal, in 1966 for the World Festival of Negro Arts. Here he could talk about the roots of his music with fierce pride. "After writing African music for thirty-five years, here I am at last in Africa!" he said.

The band played *La Plus Belle Africaine,* which Duke had written for the occasion, and he recalled the response in his autobiography: "It is a wonderful success. We get the usual diplomatic applause from the diplomatic corps down front, but the cats in the bleachers really dig it. You can see them rocking back there while we play. When we are finished, they shout their approval and dash for backstage, where they hug and embrace us, some of them with tears in their eyes. It is acceptance at the highest level, and it gives us a once-in-a-lifetime feeling of having truly broken through to our brothers."

In 1968, the band made its first visit to Latin America. As usual, Duke composed as he traveled. During the hectic schedule in South America he was writing the *Latin American Suite,* which he finished just in time for its first performance in Mexico City at the end of the tour. The next year the band played for the first time in the countries of Eastern Europe.

The next real highlight was the band's longest tour, in 1971. There were five weeks in the Soviet Union, five more in Europe, then three more in Latin America. Duke was seventy-two years old now, yet he was as enthusiastic as a schoolboy. "The anticipation of our tour of Russia in 1971 is so great that there is a risk of being consumed by it," he wrote. "Russian music in all its endlessness is too much to contemplate, so I simply try to relax, and wait to see and hear. But all those famous names are in my mind: Tchaikovsky, Rimsky-Korsakov, Glinka, Borodin, Mussorgsky, Glazunov, Scriabin, Rachmaninoff, Prokofiev, Khachaturian and Shostakovich, not forget-

ting, of course, Stravinsky. On and on and on and on . . .
I am going to breathe the same kind of air all those great
composers breathed."

These Russian composers, both past and present, were
classicists. Yet Duke had been familiar with their works
for years. He refused to classify music by type, and he
had listened to and learned from classic composers as
well as fellow jazzmen. He and Billy Strayhorn had, after
all, arranged a version of Tchaikovsky's *Nutcracker
Suite* for the band.

In Russia, Duke was wined and dined, and whisked
from one place to another, viewing all aspects of Russian
life and art. He shipped three full trunks of gifts back to
the States.

But Duke was most impressed by the respect of the
Soviet audiences: "No one ever moves from his or her
seat until the entire concert and all the encores have
been played. . . . The enthusiasm is such, and the demand for encores so insistent, that some concerts run
over four hours. Yet no one complains—not the audience,
not the stagehands, and not even the cats in the band!"

After three solid months traveling on three continents,
the Ellington band came home again. By then, Duke had
been on the road for forty years, so the routine was
familiar. Only the places and the crowds changed. Yet it
was remarkable that in so short a time Duke and his
music had gained followers in every part of the world. He
had come a long way from society dances and sign-
painting in Washington.

Duke's popularity reached a new peak in the United
States during the 1960s. The band was at the top of the

Duke Ellington greets dignitaries at the World Festival of Negro Arts in Dakar, Senegal, 1966.

Duke Ellington and his Orchestra at a Paris night club, 1969. Johnny Hodges performs at the mike. Paul Gonsalves, tenor saxophone, *sits beside piano.* Russell Procope, alto saxophone, *front row, far right.*

Ellington at the Hermitage (a palace now used as an art museum) in Leningrad, U.S.S.R., 1971.

jazz polls in magazines such as *Downbeat, Metronome,* and *Playboy,* and Duke himself often won honors as the top composer and arranger. New and better recording techniques enabled him to record the band in high fidelity. And hundreds of earlier radio transcriptions and recordings were reissued as well. As Duke's past and present work became available, people began to be aware of his remarkable history.

In concert and on record, Ellington began to feature himself at the piano more often. He played more introductions to his tunes and more solos. In the early days he had used the piano primarily as a rhythm instrument rather than as a solo voice. But in later years, as some of his major soloists left the band, he realized that he was one of the band's better solo voices. One of his albums, *Piano in the Background,* actually brought his piano into the foreground, featuring long introductions to such Ellington standards as "Take the 'A' Train," "Perdido," "What Am I Here For?" and "Happy Go-Lucky Local."

Duke's piano work grows on the listener. The first tendency is to focus on the band or some of the brass or reed soloists. Then, slowly but surely, the listener begins to get the message from the piano. Duke never had a great technique at the keyboard. But his sense of rhythm and his sense of touch made him a first-rate, innovative jazz soloist.

Duke also began to receive recognition outside the musical world. The individual awards and prizes are much too numerous to list, but they include honorary degrees from at least fifteen colleges and universities, the Presidential Medal of Freedom, which is the highest award a United States civilian can receive, the President's Gold Medal, the Legion of Honor from France, and special recognition from seven different states across the country.

There was one prize that Duke Ellington *didn't* get—a Pulitzer prize. The incident caused a small scandal. Pulitzer prizes, named for Joseph Pulitzer, who was a newspaper owner and philanthropist, have been awarded to newspapermen and writers since 1918. Since 1943, there had been an annual award for music, but the prize had been awarded only to "serious" composers of orchestral music or opera. The music committee recommended in 1965 that Duke Ellington receive a special citation for his contributions to jazz. News of its recommendation leaked out before the full Pulitzer board had voted. The board decided against the music committee's recommendation, and no special citations were awarded that year.

Ellington fans were disappointed and angry, claiming that racial prejudice was the cause of the board's refusal to give Ellington the award. Two members of the Pulitzer music committee resigned in protest.

Everyone took the incident extremely hard. Everyone, that is, but Duke Ellington. When he was asked about the incident, he said, "Fate is being very kind to me. Fate doesn't want me to be too famous too young."

Duke had just turned sixty-six. Yet he was able to look at the whole thing with tongue in cheek, a twinkle in his eye. Later he made a further comment in his autobiography: "Let's say it happened. I would have been famous, then rich, then fat and stagnant. And then? What do you do with your beautiful, young, freckled mind? How, when, and where do you get your music supplement, the deadline that drives you to complete that composition, the necessity to hear the music instead of sitting around polishing your laurels, counting your money, and waiting for the brainwashers to decide what rinse or tint is the thing this season in your tonal climate?"

Duke's comment was a put-on, an indirect way of criticizing the Pulitzer committee. But he also revealed his way of looking at himself. He was sixty-six years old, yet he still considered himself musically young. He still wanted to move forward and looked to the future with the enthusiasm of a much younger man. He accepted awards gracefully, but with a healthy detachment. For his music—not his reputation—was still the most important thing.

11

"Praise God and Dance"

At the time of the Pulitzer incident in 1965, Duke was beginning yet another phase of his long career. He had been asked by Dean C. J. Bartlett and the Reverend John S. Yaryan to compose a concert of sacred music for performance at Grace Cathedral (Episcopal) in San Francisco.

In the 1960s, churches of many denominations were showing an interest in modern music for their worship services. Folk singers and jazzmen began to create worship services in their own musical forms. Although older churchgoers often objected violently, folk and jazz masses and services were performed widely and were generally well received.

Duke welcomed the chance to compose for a church setting. "Now I can say openly what I have been saying on my knees," he commented. But, as usual, he went his own way. He didn't set a traditional church worship service to music and he didn't use traditional black spirituals and hymns. Instead, he sought to express his own personal religious faith in his own musical language.

The *First Sacred Concert*, as it would be called later, was composed like so many other Ellington works, on the road. During 1965 Duke and the band played in Europe, in Japan, and at special engagements at the White House in Washington and with the Boston Symphony at Tanglewood, Massachusetts. Yet all the time he pursued a double life, devoting his after-hours energy to his new composition. Ralph Gleason, a jazz critic and friend of Ellington, described Duke's two lives in *Rolling Stone* magazine after Duke's death: "He became so successful as a night-club performer, as a songwriter, as a *personality,* that his serious musical efforts never got the attention they deserved. He mesmerized everybody with his elegance, his charm and his melodies, and then went ahead and wrote important music behind that screen.

"He called it 'skillapooping' and defined it as the art of 'making what you're doing better than what you're supposed to be doing.' "

A kind of religious faith had meant a great deal to Duke Ellington, though he seldom worshiped in a conventional way. His mother had told him, "Edward, you don't have anything to worry about. You are blessed." And Duke came to believe that he *was* blessed. So he welcomed the opportunity to express his gratitude through his music.

The *First Sacred Concert* had its premiere on September 16, 1965. It began with Harry Carney making a six-note musical statement on his baritone sax to the words *In the Beginning God.* That was the main theme, repeated many times in many different ways. The Ellington band was accompanied by a choir, by dancers and singers, and included words written by the Duke himself, both spoken and sung.

The reaction of the listeners was almost overwhelming. Duke called it "successful beyond my wildest dreams. . . ." United Press International ran a headline that said:

DUKE ELLINGTON TALKED TO THE LORD
IN GRACE CATHEDRAL LAST NIGHT

Shortly after the first performance in San Francisco, Duke repeated the *Sacred Concert* at the Fifth Avenue Presbyterian Church in New York City. One of the important people in bringing the *Sacred Concert* to New York was Pastor John Gensel of St. Peter's Lutheran Church. Pastor Gensel served as a special minister to the jazz musicians in New York. He had heard the Ellington band for the first time in 1932 and helped form the Duke Ellington Jazz Society in the 1950s.

"Duke never spoke about a desire to do any sacred music until the early 1960s," Pastor Gensel said. "But once he became involved in it, you could see that this was the thing he loved to do most. And he did it his own way, a kind of subtle way. Without coming on and saying, 'I'm the preacher,' he was proclaiming his faith and his belief. He was really making public his private life in his relationship to God through his music and songs.

"People went wild over the concert. I was chairman of the first one here [in New York], and we priced it at two dollars a ticket so we could meet expenses. The church held 1,800 people, yet there were so many demands that we had two concerts, one at eight and the other at midnight."

In 1968, Ellington prepared his *Second Sacred Concert,* which was first performed in New York's Cathedral Church of St. John the Divine, a giant building seating more than two thousand people. He said often that he considered the *Second Sacred Concert* "the most important thing I have ever done."

The opening selection is called "Praise God," with Harry Carney on his powerful baritone saxophone setting the theme as he had in the *First Sacred Concert*. Next comes "Supreme Being," with a large choir in recitative and song, along with Jimmy Hamilton's accompaniment on clarinet. The words extol the virtues of God as the creator of the universe.

Then follows a short, but beautifully lyrical, song called "Heaven," which features the powerful and lovely voice of Swedish singer Alice Babs, and the equally powerful and lovely "voice" of the great Johnny Hodges on alto sax. The lyrics to this song are:

> Heaven, my dream,
> Heaven, divine
> Heaven, supreme
> Heaven combines
> Every sweet and pretty thing
> Life would love to bring.
> Heavenly Heaven to be
> Is just the ultimate degree to be.

The next selection, titled "Something About Believing," features the choir in singing and speaking roles. Alice Babs sings "Almighty God," accompanied by the deep, soulful, blues-oriented clarinet of Russell Procope.

Cootie Williams (who had returned to the Ellington band after a long absence) does an extraordinary solo on his muted trumpet in "The Shepherd (Who Watches Over the Night Flock)," a portrait of Pastor John Gensel. Duke wrote, "Pastor Gensel often went without, denying the needs of his own family . . . to buy food for some of the less fortunate night people. That is why we saluted him with a tonal portrait. . . . His is pure humanism and the type of unselfishness that mark a man as a true representative of God."

"The Shepherd" is followed by an up-tempo selection, "It's Freedom," featuring a crisp choral rendition of Duke's words and Johnny Hodges as the prime soloist. Some of the music of this selection is inspired by phrases Duke remembered from his old teacher and friend Willie "the Lion" Smith. The words are based on Billy Strayhorn's "four freedoms." The original four freedoms, proclaimed by President Franklin Roosevelt in 1941, were political—freedom of speech and worship and freedom from want and fear. Strayhorn's four freedoms were more personal—"freedom from hate unconditionally, freedom from self-pity, freedom from fear of doing something that would help someone else more than it does me, and freedom from the kind of pride that makes me feel I am better than my brother."

"It's Freedom" is also a special tribute to Strayhorn, who had died the year before when Duke was just beginning the *Second Sacred Concert.* It is a personal statement by Ellington about someone he loved. It ends with a solitary voice reciting the word *freedom* in twenty-one languages.

"Meditation" features a piano solo performance by Duke, tender and touching. This interlude provides a break between the first and second parts of the concert.

"The Biggest and Busiest Intersection" refers to what

Duke called the "final intersection," the gates of Heaven. "The pavement is slippery and there are all kinds of pitfalls, potholes, booby traps, and snares," he wrote in the concert notes. "The commercials that the representatives of the opposition are doing are outrageous." The number is up-tempo and features Duke's expanded percussion section.

Next comes "T.G.T.T.," which stands for "Too Good to Title." It is a moving, lyrical number featuring Alice Babs once more, this time in a wordless vocal, a device Duke had introduced in the 1920s with "Creole Love Call." Duke's notes for "T.G.T.T." explain the tune: "It violates conformity the same way, we like to think, that Jesus Christ did. The phrases never end on the note you think they will. It is a piece even the instrumentalists have trouble with, but Alice Babs read it at sight."

Two dissimilar pieces with the same theme follow next, showing Duke's ability to mix a so-called high and low feeling with the same message. Both feature the deep, resonant voice of singer Tony Watkins. The first is titled "Don't Get Down on Your Knees to Pray Until You Have Forgiven Everyone," the second, simply, "Father Forgive."

The first selection is an earthy, up-tempo number with a kind of hip lyric that bangs home its message with a wry smile:

> Have you forgiven the sinner
> Who kept you from being a winner?
> And the one who stole your bulging purse?
> Have you lost the rancor
> In your heart for the hanky-panker?
> Or for him, is there still a little curse, or worse?

After each stanza there is a refrain:

> Don't get down on your knees to pray
> Until you have forgiven everyone.

Then, with forgiveness still weighing heavily on the listener's mind, Duke moves into the soulful and serious "Father Forgive," in which he "preaches" world-wide forgiveness. Tony Watkins recites the words and after each phrase, the choir sings, "Father Forgive." The words undoubtedly spell out Duke's feelings toward man and the world:

> The hatred which divides nation from nation,
>   race from race, class from class.
> The covetous desires of men and nations
>   to possess that which is not their own.
> The greed to exploit the labors of
>   men and lay waste the earth.
> Our envy of the welfare of others.
> Our indifference to the flight of the
>   homeless and the refugee.
> The lust which uses for ignoble ends,
>   the bodies of men and women.
> The pride which leads us to trust
>   in ourselves and not in God.

The concert concludes with "Praise God and Dance." The words are first sung by Alice Babs slowly and lyrically. Then the band picks up the theme as the tempo increases. In most performances real dancers join the celebration. Duke's religious faith and his life's work playing music for dancers merge, hinting why he considered the work the most important thing he had ever done.

At the party given in honor of Ellington's seventieth birthday,
Duke shares the White House piano with Willie "the Lion" Smith.

Duke conducts a performance of the First Sacred Concert
at Fifth Avenue Presbyterian Church in New York, 1965.

Duke and the band rehearse with the choir for a performance of
the Second Sacred Concert *in Westminster Abbey, London, 1973.*

Requests for performances of the *Second Sacred Concert* flowed in from all over the world, and Duke performed it often in the next several years. He must have been pleased with it, because he didn't begin work on a third concert until 1973. He was still putting the finishing touches on it when he became ill and entered the hospital in 1974.

Whenever Duke performed either of his sacred concerts he felt that as many people as possible should share directly in the experience. He always tried to use local choirs for the chorus numbers. He would send several of his assistants ahead of the band to rehearse the local participants in the production.

The sacred concerts received few negative reviews in the press. Perhaps the critics felt they should not criticize a religious performance, or perhaps they could find no traditional basis of comparison. In any case, like much of Ellington's other music, the sacred concerts *were* unique, fitting no established category.

Taken out of context, some of the numbers in the concerts could easily be played in night clubs or dance halls. The band was certainly not out of character when performing these concerts. Duke himself wrote that "Cootie Williams growled, Cat Anderson sent notes flying around the roof, Louis Bellson made an elegant percussion declaration, Harry Carney stated the theme with power and dignity, Johnny Hodges 'sang' . . . as only he could, Paul Gonsalves swung. . . ."

Not all Ellington fans liked the marriage of religious faith and Ellington's brand of jazz. Pianist Billy Taylor preferred to see the music in the light of Duke's great recordings of the 1930s and '40s. "All these marvelous

things, '"A" Train,' and the rest, are just gorgeous
music," he said. "If one were to listen to them and then
listen to the sacred music, you can put it into a different
kind of perspective. You don't have to be religious to get
the message on the sacred concerts. They're just beautiful. And I feel the sacred concerts are very important as
American expression. Duke does use what is essentially
of this country. To me, jazz is America's classical music,
and nowhere is that better epitomized than in the music
of Duke Ellington."

The sacred concerts are part of Ellington's overall
development, but they also occupy a special place. For
they meant a little more to Duke than anything else. In
every program handed out at the sacred concerts, Duke
had a written message that concluded with a typical
positive thought.

". . . I am sure we appreciate the blessings we enjoy in
this country, but it wouldn't hurt if everyone expressed
his appreciation more often.

"We shall keep this land if we all agree on the meaning
of that unconditional word: LOVE."

The word LOVE meant much to Duke Ellington. It was
central to his life. For he loved life, loved his work, loved
the people around him, loved bringing his music and
thoughts to countless numbers of people all over the
world. And as his sacred concerts show, he also loved God
in his own individual way, and he appreciated the chance
to express it.

12

The Private Man

Duke never took a public stand on politics or politicians. But he had met and played for five presidents—Truman, Eisenhower, Kennedy, Johnson, and Nixon. And, as the 1960s came to a close, he had become a kind of musical elder statesman himself. So it came as only a minor surprise when on April 29, 1969, President Richard Nixon held a lavish birthday ball at the White House in honor of Edward Kennedy Ellington's seventieth birthday. Duke and his sister Ruth were guests of honor, and a host of celebrities, many from the jazz world, were invited.

The party was a sign that jazz had come of age. Fifty years earlier, Duke had been a dance-band manager in Washington. The word *jazz* was not familiar to most people; the idea of a black musician becoming a world celebrity seemed like nonsense. And Duke was being honored not just for his personality or for his showmanship but for his serious contributions to American music. He and his art had come a long way.

The public Ellington and his contributions were now familiar in every corner of the world. But there was another side to the man, a private side so carefully protected that even his best friends never penetrated it completely. In his later years, when Duke began piling up honors and winning awards, some sketchy details of his private life began appearing in newspapers and magazines. There were stories about his hectic schedule, his incredible work habits and pace, his upside-down, night-day existence in hotel rooms the world over.

But his privacy remained intact. In fact, he may never have allowed any one person to fully understand him. His small circle of close friends and the larger circle of those who worked with him over the years could all add some pieces to the puzzle. The full picture may never be put together.

There are hints about Duke's personality. For instance, he was fastidious and vain about his appearance and careful of his health. He underwent surgery for various ailments (hernia, kidney cyst, gall bladder), yet was basically vigorous and healthy, as his travel schedule illustrates. His friend and personal physician, Dr. Arthur Logan, once called him a "medical marvel with the physique of a man half his age." As a young man he drank great quantities of liquor without ill effects. When he decided to stop drinking in 1940, he just stopped.

Dr. Logan advised him to lose some weight in the mid-1950s, so Duke devised a diet of steak, grapefruit, salad, and black coffee with lemon. He promptly lost thirty pounds and stayed on the diet for years, later substituting hot water for the coffee. He ate steak wherever he traveled, rather than changing from one kind of food to another.

For all his good health, he was something of a hypochondriac. He carried a supply of different pills and vitamins, and called Dr. Logan from any part of the world to discuss the smallest ache or pain.

The thing he lived for and the thing that kept him going was his work. His enthusiasm seemed to have no limits. In his autobiography, Duke described a busy period in 1963: "I was writing the music for this show [*My People*, a show to be presented in Chicago] and for the Shake- spearean Festival [in] Stratford, Ontario . . . at the same time. This meant going to Stratford to work, flying to Chicago to rehearse the choirs . . . doing my one-nighters with the band in between, dashing back to New York to work with choreographers Alvin Ailey and Tally Beatty [on still another project, this one related to modern dance], returning to Stratford, and so on and on. Working from all angles at once in music and the theater was the greatest kind of fun for me."

Fun? Duke was sixty-four years old at the time.

Even when things were less hectic, Duke could seldom resist the temptation of his music. "You know how it is," he once said. "You go home expecting to go right to bed. But then, on the way, you go past the piano and there's a flirtation. It flirts with you. So, you sit down and try out a couple of chords, and when you look up it's 7 A.M."

He seemed to be continually amazed by his good for- tune. In his autobiography he wrote, "You are lucky to be hooked on something you make a living by playing—and playing with—day after day, play after play, fifty-two weeks a year. . . ."

Perhaps his work schedule was the reason he had such a passion for privacy. He didn't have the leisure hours, the vacations, the extra days and nights to spend with family and friends. So the few moments he did have had to be all *his*. He wasn't about to share them with the world at large.

It's never easy to tell what drives compulsive workers like Duke. For some, it's money. They set out to amass great fortunes and wealth. Some do it for power. They enjoy controlling the destiny of others, and perhaps carving out their own personal groove in history. Ellington's motivations were more subtle. He wanted just enough money to keep the band going and to care for his family and friends. When his music did bring handsome profits, he never really had the time to enjoy his wealth in the usual ways. And the only kind of power that interested him was his power as a composer.

Even when he was writing music, he didn't give much thought to future generations. Saxophonist Russell Procope recalled that Duke never set any long-range goals. "He was a man who wouldn't speak of the distant future," said Procope. "He always said that tomorrow would be the day. He said the best song he was going to write would be tomorrow, the best arrangement he was going to write would be tomorrow. He always looked at the immediate future, not the long-range future, and he *never* looked back over his shoulder."

Living in the here and now, optimistic about tomorrow, Duke worked with enthusiasm and zeal. Stanley Dance, who was close to Ellington and the band for years, reported, "He wrote for his own pleasure to a very great extent. He said that his biggest thrill was when he heard the band play his newest arrangement for the first time. That's true: it was a great pleasure to him."

So it wasn't money or power or a search for immortality that drove Ellington to continue his work week after

week, year after year. Perhaps it was his kind of love—
love of his music, love for his band, love of hearing his
compositions, and bringing them to new audiences. Or
perhaps it was his search for what he called a *musical
profit.*

Duke's relationship with his band members changed
over the years. In the early days, he and the other
Washingtonians were almost like one person: living,
working, and having fun together twenty-four hours a
day. But as the band grew larger Duke gave more of his
time to arranging and writing music and coordinating
the band's activities. Instead of partying with his friends,
he spent more time by himself. He slowly grew apart
from the band.

His relationship with older members of the band such
as Harry Carney, Johnny Hodges, Lawrence Brown, and
Cootie Williams was closer. Yet in later years Duke rarely
stayed in the same hotel as the band. Even though he
never kept his whereabouts secret, his separate lodgings
made him seem distant and special.

The band member Duke grew closest to in the last
years of his life was baritone saxophonist Harry Carney,
who had joined the band as a seventeen-year-old in 1927.
When the band was doing a series of one-nighters in close
proximity, Duke would always ride with Carney in
Carney's big car instead of on the band bus. He was
usually a silent passenger.

Carney remembered the way it was, in *The World of
Duke Ellington:* "Duke sleeps occasionally, but not as a
rule. He's a very good man to have along. He sits in the
front and does a lot of thinking. He'll pull out a piece of

paper and make notes. We do very little talking, but if he thinks I'm getting weary he'll make conversation so that I don't fall asleep."

To outside observers, Duke's relationship to the men had a kind of distance to it, a distance that could sometimes be seen in little ways. Pastor John Gensel, who saw the band up close during the sacred concerts in the 1960s, reported, "He was a very warm person, but . . . he was not close to most of the men in his band, in the sense of being chummy. He was the Duke; he was the *King*. He didn't interfere with the lives of the musicians, saying they had to get to bed or to rehearsal at a certain time. He just wanted them to be there when it was time to play."

Brooks Kerr also noticed Duke's detachment: "I would be surprised how he'd call men by their full names instead of their first names. If he was calling from across the room he'd say, 'Cootie Williams,' or 'Harry Carney,' instead of 'Cootie' or 'Harry.' He could be like that. I felt there were very few people who he was actually close to."

Russell Procope, who joined the band in the mid-1940s, saw Ellington from another perspective. "Duke always said he was my friend," he recalled. " 'Think of me as a friend' (which I did), 'rather than a boss or leader.' We became great friends, went places together, went out, did this and the other, but when we got out on the stage, on the platform, everybody would take care of business."

When Procope was asked if it was true that Duke wasn't as close to the musicians in his last years, Procope's answer was short and simple: "Well, wouldn't that be like any other human being?"

Duke found ways to let others take care of the practical worries such as complaints and salary problems. For many years the band had the highest payroll in the country, and discipline was generally relaxed. Still, players made complaints and demands and Duke really hated to get involved at all.

Trumpeter Clark Terry recalled an incident in the 1950s when Duke was traveling on the band bus. One of the men began to complain to Duke. When he brought up the subject of money, Duke quickly referred him to a man who had been hired to handle salaries, as Duke said, "to take this grief off me."

The musician "became even more furious, because he couldn't understand why, if he worked for Duke Ellington, he couldn't talk to Duke Ellington about . . . money. So Duke closed his eyes and went to sleep on him. He had a phenomenal knack of being able to exclude himself when he wanted."

Duke was no disciplinarian in the usual sense. He never raved and ranted or even raised his voice. Screaming didn't befit one as dignified as Duke. Nor did he ever fire anyone. The idea was repugnant to him. He felt that if things weren't working out, the player would know it and eventually leave of his own free will.

Russell Procope remembers Duke often saying, "I'm not a disciplinarian, I'm a musician." But Procope also said Duke ran the band with "an iron fist in a mink glove." His kind of discipline was just more subtle.

"Duke used strange methods of disciplining his band of unruly stars," critic Irving Townsend recalled. "I never heard him fire anybody. He tolerated the intolerable from his musicians, both because he respected their right to exercise their idiosyncrasies as he did, and because confrontation was bad for his digestion. His way of punishing a band member . . . was typically oblique. He would call upon the culprit to stand for endless solos, calling out every number that featured him, meanwhile lavishing high praise upon him, encouraging calls of 'Encore!' from the audience over the breathless protests of the victim. It was punishment indeed."

Townsend became close to Duke after the 1956 Newport Festival, when he arranged several recording sessions for the Ellington band. He gained a glimpse of the private side of the man and reported, "I soon understood that he revealed small parts of himself to many different people, thereby satisfying his need to be close to what he called his family, while at the same time denying a complete and too revealing portrait of the whole man to any one person. It would take a convention of Ellington friends and relatives, pooling their knowledge of him, to put Ellington together. And even then, like a jigsaw puzzle with missing pieces, he would emerge with patches of empty spaces in crucial places."

There was a side to Duke that longed for a more stable, conventional life. He once suddenly turned to Townsend and said, "You're a lucky man because you have a family!" But the music wouldn't allow that. So his "family" consisted of a widely scattered network of friends and relations whom he would see for brief periods whenever he was passing through. "There was no large city, no small town in the country where an old friend or an old girl or both did not wait for the next one-night visit," Townsend wrote. "These friendships . . . were renewed, enjoyed, and suspended again, usually within a twenty-four-hour period. The secret of Duke's security was constant movement. He never owned a house. A thousand hotel rooms, a thousand room-service waiters ready to push his breakfast table in on cue, a thousand loyal friends waiting to handle any local problems he might have: these made up the Ellington ménage."

Pastor John Gensel has also observed the private Ellington and provided some additional clues to the Duke's personality. "He liked to relax in an old sweater and a bandana around his head," Gensel recalled. "And whenever he saw me he'd come up and give me his traditional four kisses. I always felt extremely privileged to be in his presence. Yet he would make me feel that it was a privilege for *him* to be with *me*."

Pastor Gensel once took his entire family and a few friends to see the Duke at the Rainbow Grill in New York City. At the end of the evening when Gensel asked for the check, which was for more than two hundred dollars, he was told it had already been paid.

"I went back to Duke's dressing room and I said, 'Oh, Edward, look, you shouldn't have done that.' First, he pleaded ignorance, just said, 'What? What?' Then he said, 'Well, we all make mistakes!' He always had the words, always knew just what to say to break the tension or relax you."

But Pastor Gensel also noticed that Ellington often pulled a shade down over his thoughts: "He had a kind of mystical reserve about him where you never penetrated. There are some people you get to know and you say, 'Well, that's him! There's nothing more.' You know him in five minutes, know exactly what he is. But Duke was different. You always were left thinking, 'I wonder what he's

thinking behind the thought that's behind *that* thought,'
or 'What did he really mean by that?' or 'He's putting me
on a little.'

"He moved around people by using deep, subtle spoof-
ing whenever he needed to. And he had a certain area
within him that I for one could never penetrate. It wasn't
that he was putting me off. Instead of saying, well, it isn't
any of your business, he might just simply—by a smile or
a statement that came a little bit obliquely—indicate that
perhaps you better not pursue that thought any further."

Duke Ellington was made up of many parts, one of
them seeming to contradict another. But he put them all
together and made them work. He was at once secretive
but sentimental, loyal but unavailable, popular but
alone. He found his own happiness and contentment in a
way that would frustrate and possibly destroy a different
kind of man.

13

Endings

From the time of the Newport triumph into the 1960s the Ellington band performed brilliantly and consistently once again. Some of the stars of the past were still on hand—Johnny Hodges, Harry Carney, Lawrence Brown, and Cootie Williams. Fine players such as Cat Anderson, Willie Cook, Sam Woodyard, Paul Gonsalves, Jimmy Hamilton, and Russell Procope had been around long enough to qualify as veterans. They knew each other and what their leader expected. And Duke knew their strengths and weaknesses. This band was probably as close to the 1940 aggregation as Duke would get.

One important addition in the 1960s was Duke's son, Mercer, who joined the band as a trumpeter, and also as band manager. He took over many of the administrative and organizational duties that Duke used to handle. It made Duke very happy, and the two must have understood that Mercer would take over the entire band someday.

Mercer had studied music from an early age. After high school he attended the Juilliard School of Music, then studied composition and orchestration at New York University. After World War II he organized his own band. He didn't want to succeed on his father's name and

171

refused any help from the Duke. Like many other bands of the era, Mercer's soon folded. After that, he formed a record company, worked as a representative for a liquor distributor, and formed big bands for special engagements. He was musical director for singer Della Reese for a while, then became a successful disk jockey at station WLIB in New York City.

When Duke approached Mercer in 1964, he was sixty-five and Mercer forty-five. "I know that you've been off your horn for a long time, . . ." Duke said, "but I've decided that if any more band managers steal any more money, then I want the manager to be—you!"

Mercer joined up and remained close to his father. "I became more closely involved with him than at any other time in my life, Mercer said. "This time, it was an experience of being needed. . . ."

Duke lived as if death didn't exist. But beginning in the mid-1960s he was reminded of it more and more often.

In 1965, Billy Strayhorn became seriously ill. When he was recovering from surgery in a New York hospital, Duke called from California to discuss the *First Sacred Concert*. Duke was just working on the opening theme and he told Strays that he wanted a musical figure to represent the first four words in the Bible, *In the Beginning God.* By the time Strayhorn sent his idea to California, Duke had written one of his own. But Strayhorn thought so much like Ellington that his theme was almost exactly the same. It started and ended on the same notes, and four of the six notes were the same.

The close, almost mystical, relationship was soon to end. Strayhorn, who was only in his forties, had cancer

and never fully recovered his health. One morning in
May 1967, Duke's sister, Ruth, called to tell him that Billy
Strayhorn had died.

"I was in Reno," Duke wrote, "and I don't know what I
said, but after I hung up the phone I started sniffling and
whimpering, crying, banging my head up against the
wall, and talking to myself about the virtues of Billy
Strayhorn. Why Billy Strayhorn, I asked. Why?"

Duke continued to write and arrange at an amazing
pace after Strayhorn's death. Mercer Ellington claimed
that Duke felt he was obligated to do the work for two
men, accepting the same number of assignments as
when Strays was alive, then staying up longer and
working harder to finish them.

In 1969, Jimmy Hamilton left the band. Then in 1970,
Johnny Hodges died suddenly of a heart attack. Hodges
had been the band's most popular soloist, a musical giant
in his own right, and the centerpiece of the great Ellington sax section. In fact, Duke was writing a special solo
for Hodges in *The New Orleans Suite* when he received
word of Hodges's death. Duke was also working on his
autobiography at that time and he included a beautiful
eulogy to Hodges. Johnny's tone was "so beautiful it
sometimes brought tears to the eyes," he wrote. "So far
as our wonderful listening audience was concerned,
there was a great expectancy when they looked up and
saw Johnny Hodges sitting in the middle of the sax
section, in the front row.

"May God bless this beautiful giant in his own iden-
tity," Duke concluded.

Ellington predicted that after the loss of Hodges "our
band will never sound the same." By 1970 finding re-

Duke and veteran reedmen at a dress rehearsal for an NBC-TV special, c1965. Left to right: Billy Strayhorn, composer/arranger, Russell Procope, Harry Carney, Paul Gonsalves, Johnny Hodges, Jimmy Hamilton.

Duke discusses business with his son, Mercer, c1965.

placements for dying and departing sidemen was more difficult than ever. Brooks Kerr explained why: "Styles had changed. He couldn't find as many available people with the kind of color and tone quality he wanted. Sometimes he was lucky, like finding a Clark Terry [a modern jazz trumpeter who made a major contribution as a soloist] but there were definitely some he wouldn't have chosen in other times."

The band changed considerably in the final years, though Duke continued to take them to the far corners of the world. By 1972, drummer Sam Woodyard and trombonist Lawrence Brown had departed. The reed section still included Gonsalves, Procope, and Carney, but Duke didn't have time to integrate all the new men into the mainstream of the band. The Ellington sound was still there, but the fine balance of the band was gone. Time was catching up with them at last.

Duke continued to lose old friends. Despite the gratifications of awards, honors, and prizes, it was a time of extreme sadness. The deaths of jazz great Louis Armstrong and then Willie "the Lion" Smith in the early 1970s affected him tremendously. Armstrong went as far back in jazz as Duke himself, and Duke had loved the Lion from his early days in Washington. Then in early 1973, Duke's long-time friend and trusted physician, Arthur Logan, died suddenly. His circle of associates and friends was dwindling, but the music carried on.

Shortly after Arthur Logan's death in 1973, Duke began losing weight rapidly. He was not feeling well. When he went to a hospital for an examination, the results were shattering. Duke Ellington was suffering from lung cancer.

Yet Duke didn't give up. He continued to do what he had always done, rejoining the band and continuing his routine of writing and performing, keeping up the same pace he had kept before his illness.

In late March 1974, Duke became ill while the band was playing in Michigan. He could go on no longer. He was taken to the hospital, and for the first time in more than fifty years the Ellington band stopped working completely. It would not work again until Mercer Ellington took over the reins after Duke's death.

During those last months, Duke was in the hospital much of the time. He saw old friends and family frequently. But he kept many of his thoughts to himself.

"Duke was very courageous, very brave," said Stanley Dance. "He recognized his illness immediately for what it was. I didn't really know how he would react to something like that, but he faced it very well."

"Duke never talked about death," said Pastor Gensel. "He never talked about when he was going to die, or of any preparation for it. It was as if he was going to live all the time. In fact, I really think that he felt he was going to get well. He had this fantastic faith; he was going to go straight ahead.

"And even when he was very sick and in great pain he would still make jokes. I remember one night I was visiting him in the hospital room. He had some chicken there. He ate a little, then he said, 'You take this home, John,' and he wrapped it up and put it in a bag for me. He was more interested in me taking the chicken home and enjoying it than in lamenting or complaining about how sick he was."

Duke had been working on a third sacred concert. He was quite ill by April as his seventy-fifth birthday was fast approaching. He asked John Gensel, as a favor, to have the band perform the concert for him.

"We just couldn't get it all together in time," recalls Pastor Gensel, "but we did excerpts from it. Brooks Kerr took Duke's place at the piano, and though it wasn't played in its entirety, I hope it made him happy."

The end came quietly on May 24, 1974. Duke Ellington was gone, and the nation mourned this genius of twentieth-century American music. His funeral, in New York, was attended by some ten thousand persons, and eulogies poured in from all over the world.

President Richard M. Nixon said: "The wit, taste, intelligence, and elegance that Duke Ellington brought to his music have made him, in the eyes of millions of people both here and abroad, America's foremost composer. His memory will live for generations to come in the music with which he enriched the nation."

Other tributes came in—from musicians, critics, and hundreds of Ellington's fans, some of whom had admired him for a full half-century.

Ellington's influence on the world of jazz is both vast and hard to trace. It is almost impossible to know what "the American idiom" would be like if he had not existed. Certainly he brought a sense of elegance and musical sophistication that influenced everyone who followed after.

On the other hand, he never established a "school" of jazz. He detested categories and seemed to take delight in doing the unexpected. His music was complex and hard for inexperienced listeners to grasp, so that it took time even during the Swing Era for him to gain popularity. And his arrangements and sounds were almost impossible for others to copy. Part of his genius was that he could present such "difficult" music with such flair and showmanship that fans tried a little harder to understand his new musical ideas.

Duke himself did not go out of the way to encourage others to imitate him. Brooks Kerr has said that Duke was not a teacher. He wouldn't sit down with someone and say, "This is how it's done." And he certainly never put his musical ideas into a primer for the rest of the music world to study. There was no book of Ellington arrangements floating around. And the arrangements that were available were so geared to Duke's individual musicians that they weren't of much use to other bands anyway.

Many Ellington tunes, on the other hand, have become standards, and many of them are performed often today, by big bands and small groups. You can hear Ellington compositions daily on the radio, as well as at concerts, and on television. It's not uncommon for jazz-oriented studio bands, such as those on late-night talk shows, to play Ellington tunes during the breaks. So in that sense, Ellington the composer has left a major mark.

A few instrumentalists in the Ellington band made marks of their own. The plunger-muted "jungle" sound that Charlie Irvis, Bubber Miley, and Tricky Sam Nanton began in the 1920s was widely copied. Bassist Jimmy

Blanton, in the few short years he played, had a large influence on future bassists. Ellington gets the credit for discovering and encouraging him.

Perhaps the biggest single influence from the Ellington band was alto saxophonist Johnny Hodges. He is generally recognized as a giant on his instrument, ranking with Charlie Parker as one of the two main innovators on alto sax. Hodges's soft, relaxed lyrical style has been copied by players for decades and is still influencing young alto men everywhere.

But the Duke's greatest talent—his way of bringing out the very best in each of his band members—could not be taught. He had a kind of sixth sense that told him what a man could do best. Duke wrote music for individuals, not for instruments, and that kind of musical talent has been captured on records, remaining as a permanent part of Ellington's heritage.

How permanent his influence will be remains to be seen. Yet it's certain that many of the younger musicians who grew up listening to the Ellington sound know their indebtedness. Miles Davis, a trumpet player and a giant of jazz since the 1950s, put it simply: "We should all get down on our knees every day and thank the Duke."

One of the most significant and appropriate tributes came from Ralph Gleason, a jazz critic and friend of Ellington. Writing a farewell article about Duke shortly after his death, Gleason concluded:

"The weekend Duke died, I watched the TV news shows from the funeral parlor and the church with all those thousands who came from all over to mourn him, and I could not cry for Duke. He was out there living every minute like a teenager right up to the last few months. He had been everywhere, seen everything, knew everybody, and all his adult life he had the one thing he wanted most—his orchestra to play his music. And what music! As the French poet Blaise Cendrars said, 'Such music is not only a new art form, but a new reason for living.' "

The Duke was dedicated to living music—an art form that never stops growing and changing. He was proud of his contribution to the music of his own times, whether it was called "jazz," or "the music of black people," or "the American idiom." But if his music lives on even when that of other jazz greats is forgotten, it will be for the reason his old friend and drummer Sonny Greer once expressed.

"Duke was one of the few men you'll ever meet who could put his dreams on paper," Greer said.

And in doing so, Edward Kennedy "Duke" Ellington made us all a little bit richer.

Index

Page numbers in italics refer to photographs.

Author's Note: Duke Ellington spent many hours in the recording studio during the course of his long career. These are but a few of the records available today that bring the Ellington years back to life.

Discography

Black, Brown and Beige, Columbia, JCS-8015

Concert of Sacred Music, RCA, LSP-3582

Duke Ellington's Second Sacred Concert,
    Prestige, P-24045 (2 records)

Early Ellington, Everest Archives, 221

The Early Years, Everest Archives, 249

Ellington at Newport, Columbia, CS-8648

Greatest Hits, Columbia, CS-9629

In a Mellotone, RCA, LPM-1364

The Indispensable Duke Ellington,
    RCA, LPM-6009 (2 records)

Piano in the Background, Columbia, CS-8346

This Is Duke Ellington, RCA, VPM-6042 (2 records)

The World of Duke Ellington,
    Volume I, Columbia, G-32564 (2 records)

The World of Duke Ellington,
    Volume II, Columbia, KG-33341 (2 records)

The Yale Concert, Fantasy, 9433